AND HOW SHE GREW

Also by Stanton Delaplane:

THE LITTLE WORLD OF STANTON DELAPLANE

DELAPLANE IN MEXICO

(with Robert de Roos)

GREW
SHE
HOW
AND

by Stanton Delaplane

COWARD-McCANN, Inc.

New York

*There are a number of books on how to raise chil-
dren. This is not one of them.*

*While my child was growing up, I wrote a daily
column. It is a day-to-day, hot-off-the-press record of
how we grew.*

*It took a large stage and a cast of characters. You
cannot raise children without bankers, builders, dogs,
cats, bees, a set of home plumbing tools and an occa-
sional dry martini.*

*This book is not about how to raise children. It is
about how to survive.*

As Dr. Benn Reyes puts it so well in The Years from
Five to Ten:

*"This is the docile age. The child is seldom diso-
bedient. In fact, the reverse is true, the child, oriented
upon the parents, seeks approval. Such things as
thumb-sucking are easily overcome by the understanding parent."*

*I raised my child by the books. I was a Monday
morning quarterback to Spock and tried to outguess
Gesell.*

*Without reading a blooming line, my child out-
guessed us all.*

AND HOW SHE GREW

1

*D*O you want to hear some rugged news?" she said.

"No thank you," I said shortly. "I want to hear lovely, pleasant news. I would like to hear news that you have become a child movie star with a five-year contract. Or a Woodbury bride."

"A terrible thing happened," she said unheeding. "First Mike chewed an ear off the goat."

"What goat?" I said shaken out of my copy of *Range Romances.* "Have we got a goat?"

"It is the goat down the street," she said. "Mike chewed his ear off and then the police came. I was scared. I said 'Please, please, don't take Mike to jail—' "

"Start at the beginning," I said.

One thing I will say for that child, she puts a catchy lead on her material. I do not care to have my boxer, whose name is Carmichael, chewing ears off anything. And I certainly do not care for any attention from the Johnny Nabs.

9

"Well," she said smugly, "there was this goat. And I was walking along. And I didn't go near the goat or anything. And when Mike went up to the goat, I told him not to. But he wouldn't mind. And then they started fighting, you know? And he chewed his ear off. And then the policeman came" —here the voice goes into soap opera—"and then I cried and cried—"

"Skip the violins," I said. "Did he really chew his ear off?"

"Well, he sort of licked it off," she said cautiously.

My boxer, Carmichael, places both loving paws squarely upon my clean shirt and looks me in the eye.

"I went to dancing school," says the young lady. "And there was this boy, you know? And he bowed at me. And then there was this girl. And she was so mean. Real bossy and so mean and—"

"Stop," I say wiping my eyes. "It is too tragic."

"Then I bruised myself real bad," she says pulling up her dress to show me.

"Terrible," I say. "Didn't Helen Trent bruise herself? And then she had her leg cut off or something?"

"Why no," she says. "It was the doctor. He had to do this operation, you know? And then she said she had to go to Hollywood and—"

"Never mind," I say. "I can't bear it. It is all so grievous."

Ninety pounds of boxer has climbed into my lap. The better to see me, my dear.

"Steak," he says drooling. "Two big steaks. One for you and one for me. How about it, pal?"

Mr. Clyde Beatty has a soft job. Mr. Beatty gets in a cage full of lions and tigers and such. People at the circus watch

Mr. Beatty snapping his whip and poking the cats with a kitchen chair. They scream like everything. The people, I mean. And Mr. Beatty for this collects a good deal of cabbage.

Every once in a while I enter a cage full of small girls. I get paid nothing for this because most people do not realize how dangerous it is. I do not have a whip (though I am thinking of buying one). And I do not carry a kitchen chair lest one of the young ladies take it away and belt me with it.

People do not scream with delight. Or if they do, I cannot hear them. For the young ladies do a great deal of screaming themselves.

"Mr. Delaplane, Jill is kicking me under the table."

"Ladies, ladies," I say. "*Shuddup!*"

As of Easter Sunday, I embarked with three of these young ladies to a fancy hotel. The management had set up a breakfast special for children and two ladies in rabbit suits ran about the floor and shook hands with everybody. An orchestra was running up a few waltzes and there was a great deal of egg decoration.

Among my guests was a young lady personally known to me for the past eight years and I gave her genteel instructions before leaving.

"One fast remark out of you," I said, "and it's the Oregon boot."

"Yes, Father," she said meekly.

Well, as Mr. Beatty once remarked in an interview: "Never turn your back on a tiger."

I tell you it was heart-warming to look over my guests. Everybody in white gloves and organdy. All with purses, pearls, all combed and brushed.

"Ladies," I said. "Your orders if you please."

"We will have eggs Benedict," they said.

"Oh no," I said cunningly. "The creamed chicken is much better." (The reason I say this is because creamed chicken is much easier to mop up off of organdy than egg. There was enough egg decoration around anyway.)

"Eggs," they chorused.

We settled for chicken. ("Let 'em know who's boss right away," Clyde Beatty used to say.)

Now I do not know how these things come apart. For I am sure there was no warning. One minute we are all in organdy and the next minute in tears.

"We want to hunt eggs," they said.

"Now girls, we will all hunt eggs later," I said. "First we will all scoff up our breakfast like all the nice people around us. Then we will hunt eggs."

The faces began to come apart like so many plates cracking.

"Those other children are hunting eggs," they said. And so they were. A pair of little gun jumpers, digging them out with great squeals from the floral center in the Palm Court.

"Look," I said desperately, "there must be thousands of eggs here, for this hotel is very rich and an egg here or an egg there is of no consequence. Wouldn't you like to finish your chicken?"

I regret to say it was my own young lady who came to pieces first. It starts with a working of the mouth and in a minute tears are skiing down the cheeks.

"We want to hunt eggs. WAHHHHHH!"

Well, there is nothing much you can do. I retired to sulk with a bottle of beer.

I saw my charges a few times thereafter. The combed hair

was down over the eyes and the organdy was somewhat crushed. At times I was called upon to settle disputes. Who should get the one cookie that was chocolate? Certain persons had got chocolate rabbits while others had chocolate eggs. Was that fair?

It was worse than a labor negotiation.

It was sometime in the afternoon that I got them all aboard the car again for delivery home.

"It is very quiet in the back seat, ladies," I said. "What are you doing?"

"We are making fudge, Mr. Delaplane."

So they were. And the way you make fudge is like this: You take your bag of Easter chocolate rabbits and eggs and whatever else you have. And you squeeze the bag from the top and it sort of smashes it all together in a fudge.

Of course at a certain point the seams of the bag give way and the fudge comes out like toothpaste. What fudge does to organdy, you wouldn't believe. And it never comes off of seat cushions unless you apply the seat of newly cleaned trousers.

Which is why I wonder why all the fuss about Mr. Clyde Beatty.

I am more the Frank Buck type myself. Bring 'em back alive. Which is what I did but it was touch and go all the way.

In the warm days of summer, the *Ladies' Home Journal* gets a good deal of my attention. I am always anxious to see what ladies will think of next and this is the way to find out.

The ladies' magazine is trying to find a Homemaker of Tomorrow. And they have been quizzing a lot of teen-age dolls who wouldn't know a frying pan from a sheriff's pistol.

This is hardly the way to get to the bottom of a quiz program. And I think they should ask me. To wit:

"If a baby sucks his thumb, the homemaker should: (A) punish him. (B) Divert him by giving him something with which to play. (C) Ignore the matter completely."

This is a pretty good question. And I will be glad to answer it from experience. My daughter has been sucking her thumb ever since she first saw it. I can tell you a thing or two about this matter.

When the first thumb chewing starts, you should read a good book.

This book will say:

"Thumb-sucking often denotes an emotional need . . ."

You can spend a lot of time and patience working with this kind of book. It is useless.

My personal opinion is that babies suck their thumbs because they arc blooming well bored. They suck their thumbs because they are too young to go out and hold up a bank.

In the interests of science I have asked my daughter: "Honey, why do you suck your thumb?"

"Because I like to," she said candidly.

And let me tell you, I have threatened that child with the lash. I have offered her the rack and the Iron Maiden. That is *all* I can get out of her. I really believe it is not such a bad answer at that.

If what the books say is true, how come no bright moppet has told the writer, "Sir, I suck my thumb because I have an emotional need"?

I have looked over these books completely. Not a direct quote in the bunch. Just opinions by the writer.

If I had brought in such material when I was a young molder of public opinion, the city editor would have flung me out the door. We had to document our stuff.

As to this matter of giving the child something else— divert him. I used to divert my daughter by various things. I gave her toys.

She grew very agile with her pinkies. Being able to hit me left-handed with a toy train without once removing the thumb from her mouth.

I put on little plays for her and made comical faces. She laughed heartily. She learned to laugh *around* her thumb.

Once I feared the thumb might be growing there and I pulled it out forcibly. She was about three then and had a kick like a mule. I can still feel it. By the time I got up off the floor, she had put the thumb back in the holster and was looking at me coldly. Like Gary Cooper looks when he is stalking his man thataway.

"GITCHER THUMB OUTA YER MOUTH!"

She sneers at me. She is so handy with that thumb that she can shift it to one corner of her mouth and sneer with the other side.

What I say is if you give this problem to a teen-ager, you won't get Tomorrow's Homemaker out of it. What you are going to get is a raving maniac.

That quiz kid probably has to get her own thumb out of her mouth to answer the questions.

The late Mr. Eddie Guest, who was named the greatest poet in the world by the late Mr. Henry Ford, once remarked in a syndicated way: "It takes a heap o' livin' in a house t' make it home."

I have investigated this statement thoroughly and can now state that it is true. If you live through it.

It was nearly a year ago that I approached my banker with hat in hand and an eye full of stardust.

"What kind of house do you wish to build?" he said.

"A mere cottage," I said. "A wilderness retreat. A house by the side of the road where the race of men go by."

"Hmm," said the banker, "has it got a bathroom downstairs?"

"Why, I scarcely gave it a thought," I said. "Everybody in my household being hale and hearty and able to climb stairs like a blooming antelope if necessary."

"You gotta have a bathroom downstairs," said the banker. "It improves the resale value."

"But I don't want to sell it," I cried. "I want to live in it."

"Ah, but we may want to resell it," said the banker, stroking the gold nuggets on his watch chain.

Well, dear hearts, this is what occurs when modern man seeks to build a nest.

This is not the way I had pictured it at all. I had pictured a sturdy mansion arising amid the ring of axes. We would fell trees—or anyway, a strong man hired for the purpose would fell trees. Or maybe I would lay in a barrel of cider and all the jolly neighbors would come around and fell trees.

Oh, it would be a gay time. With the broad-shouldered frontiersmen singing in the wilderness. And all the merry wives unpacking the pickles and cuffing the children.

"You have an architect?" said the banker.

"I have," I said sullenly. "A genial gent has drawn some things on blue paper. Though for the life of me I do not know what."

"Why, then," cried the banker merrily, "you are practically in your own home. We call it your home," he said, "though it is actually our home. But we bankers are sentimental folk. And if you play your cards right, it will be your home. In about fifty years."

A good many things have happened to our home. I call it our home because I am sentimental too. My home and the banker's.

My friendly builder got me on the blower this early A.M.

"Did you ever think how nice it would be if your windows were painted white?" he said.

"Why, Walter," I said, "I love white. Especially in shirts and on brides. But I thought the windows were to be natural wood."

"A slight mistake has occurred," said the builder gloomily. "Somebody got loose with the paint pot and not only painted your house but the windows also."

Immediately, I got the banker on the pipe.

"Something has happened to our house," I said. "In fact, to your house. There has been some paint spread around which may cost you a pretty penny. And I assume, being a banker, you have many pretty pennies. For I have always heard that bankers are a frugal lot."

"Why, my boy," he said, "when these things happen, it is your home. And you must strive to do better and watch the painters and harry the carpenters.

"It is only our house," said the banker, "in case you fail to meet the monthly payment with the old ready."

"But, sir," I cried, "there was the extra payment for removing the large rock which was cunningly hid beneath the garage floor. Also, the matter of a grand for a little old change of plans. Soon I shall not have the wherewithal to live."

"That is the way it goes," said the banker. " 'It takes a heap of living—' "

A suburban householder is faced almost daily with command decisions. It is a good thing I am an orderly and executive type.

The Siamese cat has come forward with a delicate problem.

"I'm in love!" she screamed. "Meeeooowr! Love!"

I must say that I handled this in an adult way. I did not sit around telling this cat:

"You are too young to know your own mind." Or, "How can you be sure, my dear? That tomcat is old enough to be your father."

For one thing, a Siamese involved in the tender feelings of spring is pretty fearsome. They go yowling up trees and they rip the furniture to ribbons. When a Siamese feels thataway, everybody else should go every whichaway.

I therefore consulted some Siamese-owning neighbors who advised me to fling this shameless Jezebel into a place where they raise Siamese cats.

And so on a Sunday, I drove the lady over. The back seat full of mournful yowls and flying cat hair. It was the first time I had ever been inside a cattery. And it is quite an experience.

The front yard was full of Siamese tomcats. Standing around the drugstore and whistling at passing lady cats.

"Is she fully seal point?" said the cat lady. "We have an excellent seal point male for $20."

"That is not the idea, ma'am," I said. "What would my cat do with $20? If the gentleman wants to give her a little old present. Say a mink shrug. We would accept. But I assure you—"

"The commercial fee is $20 which you pay me. The expense of boarding and so on, you know," said the cat lady. "What did you think?"

"I thought we would introduce her around. Maybe give a catnip tea. Then they could call on her at suitable times. With little presents such as candy and flowers which is all a nice girl may accept. I had in mind a long engagement suitably chaperoned and—"

"Then you don't know Siamese," said the cat lady.

This is true. I have not made a study of Siamese. Being engaged in other lines of work and molding public opinion and so on.

It also appears that you cannot simply take your Siamese to the cat lady. And in later years sit comfortably around the fireside with Siamese kittens rollicking up and down the lace curtains.

It seems my Siamese has no use for other Siamese.

She is madly in love with a moth-eaten alley cat who has been sneaking around the house every time my back was turned.

This true love, I believe, is a part-time burglar and probably a sherry bum to boot. But to my Siamese he is a cat John Wayne. Whenever he shows up she is primping and washing her face and full of tail switch.

To her, the cat lady's Siamese are Ivy League longhairs.

What my cat wants is a cat with hair on his chest.

"We put the two kitties in separate wire-screen boxes and let them talk to each other and get acquainted first," said the cat lady professionally.

"What do they talk about?" I said, whipping out my notebook.

"It seems to calm them down."

"You mean she may learn to forget that bum who has been hanging around the house? Like sending your daughter to Europe to get over a mad passion for the chauffeur who later turns out to be a rich college boy on a lark? Like the movies?"

"It is a matter of directing her interest in other directions. We can only hope it is not too late," said the cat lady.

My child lives in an age of mechanical marvels and a Space Cadet hat with a whirligig on it that spins when she runs. It is made of plastic.

Electric gadgets turn our heat on and off. A gasoline engine whisks her to school. Television provides her with her daydreams and nightmares. She is practically untouched by human hand—the new citizen of our atomic world.

Yet I perceive nostalgia creeping back through the AC floor plug. I wonder if we know what we are doing.

What I mean is the number of ads that offer gadgets to ungadget us.

The further science takes us on a cyclotronic whirl, the more we sneak back to the velocipede.

I am indebted to *Gourmet* magazine this month. The issue with the "how to have a luau in your own back yard" article by Trader Vic. I find my evidence.

Do you know that for $65 you can have a home grinder so you can grind your own flour and bake your own bread?

"Honest bread begins with honest flour," it says. "And honest flour begins at home . . ."

Think of that. You don't have to go down to the store and buy a loaf of bread. How do you know *that* flour is not dishonest? Maybe it never went through a loyalty quiz. No sir, now you can buy honest grain and churn it at home.

For $19.95 you can purchase a Yoghurt Master. "It takes the guesswork out of yoghurt made at home."

This is a buy and a bargain. If there is anything annoying, it is guessing about yoghurt.

This is the pioneer coming out in us. The hand shading the eyes. The covered wagon heading West with the homemade yoghurt bubbling under the axle.

We can do all sorts of things at home again. Grind our own flour, our own pepper, coffee and hamburger. I have a gadget that chops my highball ice electrically. But I am working on something to get us further back. I am working on a gadget that wraps the ice in an old dish towel and hammers it. With one in every ten strokes hitting your thumb.

For a long time I did not realize how far we had come off the road our grandmothers trod in sunbonnet with a milking pail.

I noticed that whenever I opened the can of Hills Bros., my daughter was around.

"Let me smell it," she demanded. She liked the little whoosh of coffee smell that comes out when the seal breaks.

It occurred to me that this growing child had never known the satisfying odor of my own youth. The smell of coffee in the grinder filling the house in the morning.

"My dear," I said, "forgive your poor old electrified parent. I see that I have failed to direct your eager footsteps in the pioneer path I cleared for you.

"How well I remember, dear heart, the brisk smell of

coffee and buffalo steaks when I was riding the Pony Express."

"The girls at school say you never killed any Indians and never were a cowboy. Anyway, where did you buy coffee?" she said.

"A lot those little chatterboxes know about it," I cried. "Coffee we ground out of beans—"

"Ha, ha, ha," she said. "Coffee out of beans. Coffee comes in cans. And anyway I don't like beans."

I bought an electric coffee grinder and a selection of Mocha and Java and turned it on for a small board of small inquirers.

The first try blew a fuse. And the second try burned out some kind of coil.

It was a very dismal failure and nobody seems to listen to my tales of the Great Plains and the Pony Express and the Indian princess who was daffy over me.

Naturally I had it repaired. The man said the trouble was that we had the television and the electric ice chopper and the electric mixer and the washing machine and the freezer and the vacuum cleaner on at the same time.

Since I cannot live without most of these things going, I have just sort of given up coffee grinding for the time being. I am a fairly pioneer type anyway. I open my coffee cans by hand.

Comes the golden autumn day when all good men must come to the aid of the car pool.

My car pool this year is lively. We have three young ladies in the seven-year-old bracket and two *femmes fatales* of eleven. The eleven-year-olds sit in front with me and discuss what boys they would not be caught dead with, not for *anything!* The seven-year-olds sit in the back and take the jack apart. The jack is an expensive and complicated thing, guaranteed to raise a truck.

When three seven-year-olds get through investigating it, it develops hernia and isn't supposed to lift anything.

The car is a station wagon. This is fortunate because it gives us plenty of room to take the boxer dog. He sits in the very back and tries to climb through the windows and murder other dogs we pass en route. We have a lively car pool.

All my car pool people wear the gingham dresses and green pinafores of Dominican young ladies.

People who pass us know that we are on our way to school. The ladies are freshly scrubbed and, at a distance, I imagine I look thoughtful and kindly.

"Look at the nice man and the little girls on their way to school," they say. They should be inside the car.

"Mr. Delaplane. Did you hear about the boy who was murdered?"

"No, tell me."

"Well, there was this man, you know. And he took this boy and he cut him all in pieces. Like a chicken!"

"Where was this?"

"I don't know. Somewhere."

"Well, where did you hear about it?"

"I don't know. Somewhere. Do you know my aunt? Well, she visited us and she had to sleep in my grandmother's bed and she said if she had to sleep there any more she wouldn't visit us. And my grandmother said she was a stuck-up old thing."

"What's that got to do with the boy cut up like a chicken?"

"Nothing. I got cut up under my big toe. Would you like to see it?"

My car pool covers about 10 miles. We have five stops. We pass beagles and schnauzers and Pomeranians and collies and boxers.

My boxer rages up and down in his area like a lion. The noise is terrific!

The seven-year-olds cheer him on. "Kill him! Get him, Mike! Sic 'em, boy!"

The cheery young ladies in the front seat are too old for this sort of small play. They discuss boys.

I know they would not go out with Richard. Richard has bands on his teeth. The fact that Richard has not asked them or the fact that they have bands on *their* teeth has nothing to do with the problem. They live in a dream world.

"Even if he begged me, I wouldn't. Ugh!"

"Why not?" I have seen Richard. Aside from the fact that he is a vacant-looking child whose mouth hangs open, he does not seem bad.

"I just wouldn't. He's real dumb. He could send me flowers or *anything*. I wouldn't."

Poor Richard.

We have music in our car pool. We turn on the radio real LOUD. We have a girl assigned to run up and down the dial.

"There! That one! Stop there. Oh, that's real neat!"

"WHAT IS THAT ONE?" I yell.

"THAT'S 'ROCKET DAVY CROCKETT!' OH, IT'S REAL NEAT!"

"COULD WE HAVE IT A LITTLE LOWER? Thank you."

"Mr. Delaplane. Did you hear about the lady and, I forget

where, but it was in the paper and her husband chopped her head off with a big ax?"

We have a lively car pool. Murder and Richard and dogs and "Rocket Davy Crockett." It is no wonder that people give us such friendly smiles when we pass by. Smiling Jack and all the little Rippers.

On days when I drive the car pool to school, I am expected to perform. It has put a strain on my memory. To say nothing of imagination.

My car pool is made up of young ladies, age seven to eleven.

"Tell us about when you were a policeman," they say.

"I shall never forget my days with the Mounties," I say. "It was bitter cold, 60 below. I was on the trail of a bank robber known as Sad-Eyed Sam."

Ah, but that was in the old days. Today I simply answer:

"My dears, I never was a policeman. I have great respect for the Johnny Nabs as well as all law and order. But I have not joined forces with them."

"But you said last week—"

"Hush. What if the Republican Central Committee should hear you?"

Here is a statement I run across in the daily journals. And it shows we journalists must be on our toes.

"Americans opened 42 billion cans last year—259 for every man, woman and child in the country."

This is released by the can people. I do not know about their figures. Probably there were 42 billion cans opened. But they were not opened by women and children. That is the fallacy. We must watch out for these things.

Most cans are opened by the lord and master. The squire of the household comes home from a hard day at the office. He puts on his slippers and begins to engage in thoughtful work—you know, reading the paper or catching a TV program.

Pretty soon there is a cry for help from the kitchen.

"My love," says the lady of the house, "can you open this can for me?"

I do not know how these things are worked out on timing. But this cry comes just as the good guy is about to scrag the bad guy.

The gent must then arise and wrestle with the can. The lady does not want the can opened. She wants company.

"You do it so well," she says. "Now tell me everything that happened downtown today."

This is the direct approach. Ladies have worked out another fascinating way to break their loved ones loose from the day's rest.

A lady takes a can and puts it on the slippery sink. She then takes one of those sharp-pointed can openers and puts the point on top of the can.

Does she give it a sharp blow and puncture the can?

No sir. She begins to press. In order to get more leverage, she puts her face down on her hands. "Ugh, ugh," she says.

The gent looks up. The can is skittering all over the sink and his storm-and-strife is about to lose an eye. It is the most distracting thing in the world.

"Good grief!" he screams. "You want to cut your throat? Give me that opener."

The lady relinquishes it. She gives him a little helpless smile.

"You do it so much better," she says. Good guys lose.

The odd thing about this is that madam usually has about three can openers strapped to the wall. Foolproof jobs where you attach the can and give a couple of turns to the crank.

But ladies claim they cannot use these things. Not if they can get the breadwinner out of the easy chair.

"It seems so complicated," they say helplessly. "Now, don't bother. You just stay where you are and rest."

Meanwhile she is about to gouge an eye. It is like trying to rest with somebody playing Russian roulette in the next room.

There is also the sardine can. The sardine can is equipped with a key welded to the backside. When you put this key on the tab and start to wind, the metal tab breaks off.

"I don't know how it happened," says the lady. "Why don't they make them so you can open them?"

The gentleman then goes to work with a screw driver and a pair of pliers.

Coffee cans are also a puzzle. By the time madam admits she is whipped, the key is all wound up on a sharp snarl of tin ribbon. I estimate the time for fixing this at five perspiring minutes.

"You might as well sit down at the table," says the lady. "The peas will be done in two minutes. Thanks for opening the can."

We should point out that this happens only 259 evenings of the year. The other 106 evenings you can rest. Or open your own 259 cans.

As if I didn't have enough problems, the Siamese cat has moved her kittens out of the garage. She favors my shirt drawer but has settled, a little grumpily, for a carton box in the bathroom.

I must be careful brushing my teeth or I drop water on the kittens. It makes the Siamese nervous. Nervous as a cat in fact. One drop of water and she has to go over these kittens from head to tail.

Fortunately I was out of town when these kittens arrived. Both the Siamese and I were in a state of nervous exhaustion waiting for them.

I had pictures of myself delivering these kittens personally. Something like the kindly police sergeants who are always delivering babies in taxicabs at the height of the rush hour.

I wouldn't know anything about delivering kittens if they were gift-wrapped for Christmas. All I could think of was stimulants.

I kept a bottle of brandy handy. With an eyedropper for the Siamese. A glass for me. I thought we might need it.

Well, it turned out the Siamese attended to the whole matter herself.

For five days she was constantly up and around. Straightening their pillows and checking to see that they did not have two heads.

On the sixth day, she brought them up one by one and tried to put them in the shirt drawer.

"You stay with them," she said. "I'm worn out."

However, she is just like any other mother. She sticks around trying to tell me what to do.

"Keep them warm. Keep them dry. Don't do that! You'll smother them!"

Pretty soon she is back in the box. Roughing them up with

her tongue and complaining that it's impossible to get decent help these days.

These kittens did *not* turn out Siamese. Not by any stretch of the imagination.

One is black. One is sort of striped. One is gray.

The gray one looks exactly like a swaggering tomcat that lives down the street.

Anyway, he was around the house all the time while the romance season was on. Since the kittens arrived, we haven't seen hide nor hair of him.

I think I saw him hanging around a wharf saloon the other night. But I couldn't be sure. I think he was passing out cigars.

The Siamese takes this bravely though.

She is willing for me to go to work and support the kittens.

"You know how it is," she says scuffing a paw in the dirt.

The kittens are world travelers already. The Siamese moves them constantly.

She moves them so often, she sometimes forgets where she puts them.

Anyway, it is soon mealtime. It is dinner time almost all the time with these kittens. They have shrill voices. When they start to yell, she locates them. After they are fed, she moves them again.

I have chopped up cashmere sweaters for this addlepated female. I have lined Christmas boxes with an imported English coat. Only a little worn at the elbows.

Nothing seems right. You would think there was a law that all kittens must be raised in a shirt drawer. When I haul them out, she spits at me. You would think that I had declared against motherhood.

I have been cat-sitting for eight weeks now. Ever since she

showed up with some vague tale of finding the kittens under a cabbage leaf.

An excellent mother, but she does not intend to sit with her offspring when there is a built-in kitten sitter like me around.

When evening rolls around, I put out enough cat food to feed a tiger. This cat sits around watching while the kittens eat until they wobble. Then she puts on a terrific act.

She howls and staggers as though she had just come out of Starvationville.

"I'm dying," she screams. "Dying of hunger."

I then shoo the kittens out the door and give this cat a big dish of horse meat. Does she eat it? Ha! She fills her mouth and takes it out and stuffs more in the kittens.

Well, it is like pouring pablum into a baby. She feeds them until they are glassy-eyed. Then she brings them back in the house and leaves them with me.

"Keep an eye on them," she says. "I'll be back in a minute."

She does not return until dawn. It is my opinion this cat spends her evenings sitting on a bar stool. Telling everybody how her husband deserted her and what a good cook she is and how she would love to settle down again with the Right Man.

There is something funny going on.

It takes a good deal of scratch to educate children today. But it takes a good deal more to dress them for it. The original cost is not the end. It is the upkeep that stings.

I cannot remember that anybody dressed me up much to get back behind the books.

"Put your shoes on," they said. "Put on your shoes and go to school."

It is different in my household. We cannot go to school without a car coat. A car coat is a special coat you wear in little sports cars. And even if you go to school courtesy of the neighbor's pickup truck, you must arrive in a sports coat.

There is also the matter of new ball-point pens. And paper. And binders. And books.

We get enough of these things each year to outfit an insurance office.

We get pens that will write under water. Pens that will write on slick paper. Also pens to replace lost pens. I keep the stockholders happy in the pen companies. I support them.

We have come a long way from my simple days.

When I was going to school, we bought pen points. And a pen wiper. (My writing is pretty bad. But that is what I got a typewriter for.)

"Anyway, I got these pen points and pen wiper and I *kept them in my desk!*" That is what I tell my offspring.

She does not have a desk, I guess. She keeps her pens in a leather case. Like a banker. In this way, she has about three miles each way each day to lose them.

A lot of glamour has gone out of the little red schoolhouse with such Fancy Dan doings, it seems to me. I do not recall that we needed a diplomat's briefcase to get our books home.

What we got was a strap. You strapped your books into this strap. And you swung them around your head. And you picked a likely smaller boy. And you hit him over the noggin. Bang!

As for dressing, I never heard of a car coat. Your mother

dressed you up and said: "Now keep that overcoat on, do you hear?"

You then set off. and around the block, you took off the coat and hid it. You untied your shoelaces and tied them again in the fashionable way of the moment. You took off your tie and stuck it in your coat.

Then you made sure you had a good supply of rubber bands in your foxy pocket and you were ready. The school supplied the ink.

The young lady of whom I speak is a slick article. She is almost as slick as her modest parent. Not quite. But almost.

I have been reading her latest school theme, entitled "Hawiia For Me."

I assume this means "Hawaii" for I took her there for one mad whirl of coconut hats and pineapple in a bygone year.

HAWIIA FOR ME she puts at the top.

> We had lots of fun when we went to Hawiia last month. We like the boat ride. And when we got there we were loded with leis.
>
> We like to see the pretty dance. We saw cocanut trees and hat.
>
> We saw people drinck a drinck out of a cocanut.
>
> I had a childs drinck with a cocanut.
>
> I went to pearl harber and got a boat and rode arround.
>
> I went in the water at the beach. I put my toes in because I thoulht it was cold but it was warm and shwoll.
>
> I walked to a rath.
>
> I allso take sufferboard rideing but cept on falling in so I quik.
>
> But all in all it was fun.

Well, I have looked this over with a good deal of pride. The kid is chipped right off the old block and tackle. Including the spelling.

The construction I find excellent. We start right off in Hawaii.

We get loaded with leis. Romance.

We belt a little belt out of the coconut. South Seas stuff.

She had a child's drink out of a coconut. Very sound and moral.

She went to Pearl Harbor and rode around. Patriotic.

She went in the water at the beach and only put her toes in because it might be cold. Suspense stuff.

She walked out to a raft. Brave but modest too.

She took surfboard riding but fell in and quit. Athletic. But not enough to drive off the men. A nice type for the home.

"All in all it was fun." Happy ending.

Well, I begin to see the value of education which has required a modest portion of my income.

It is quite possible this moppet may develop to the point she could take over my daily stint with the arts. Thus leaving me free to go to "Hawiia" and "drinck a drinck out of a cocanut."

I do not mind admitting that Hawiia Is For Me too. If a substitute jockey could be put aboard the typewriter.

I find no mention of certain rare happenings at Waikiki. Such as a public kiss by a golden youth of nine years. She being then an impressionable seven. So I assume she has edited this out. As must all of us with some mighty fine copy. We write for the family trade.

I see no note of sadness. And naturally there were mo-

ments of tears. At bedtime and suchlike tragedies which in-
fringe upon our youth.

This seems to me a gay and illiterate piece. In the highest
traditions of the newspaper dodge. And I foresee this young
genius giving stomach flutters to many a copyreader with
spelling alone.

I do not know what television is doing to Hollywood. I am
too busy contemplating what TV is doing to me. I was sitting around home the other night with Mr. Irving Hoffman,
the Broadway column gentleman. And we auditioned the
young lady who shares my TV emotional life.

We agreed that TV should be written (as cynics insist)
for the eight-year-old mind. Because the eight-year-olds
truly own the 27-inch screen.

"Walter Windshield!" screamed the young lady.

"What?" we said in alarm.

"Walter Windshield will be on TV tonight," she said.

"Walter Winchell." I translated for Mr. Hoffman. "She likes
Walter Winchell."

Now the reason all this must be relayed is because I am a
very smart person. I was not behind the door when the
brains were passed out. My TV set is silent.

For some time the guardians of law in the lawless West
volleyed and thundered through my household. Then, with
a simple attachment of a long cord and a plug-in box, the
situation was solved.

Now two sets of earphones plug into the plug-in box.
A switch throws off the sound in the television and pipes it
into the childish ears. And mayhem is committed and In-

dians are massacred and people die horrid deaths quite silently.

"Why do you like Walter Winchell?" said Mr. Hoffman. Mr. Hoffman is an inquiring reporter.

"WHAT?"

There is a small problem with the plug-in system. The child's ears are filled with loud weeping and wailing and pistol shots and the clatter of cavalry. She speaks loudly so that we may hear above this silent uproar. Consequently her voice booms out like a football coach at practice.

"Why do you like Walter Winchell?" said Mr. Hoffman. "Walter," said Hoffman to me, "gives away ponies. It is his pitch to keep the kids listening to the program because his time bucks up against the Lone Ranger.

"Do you like the ponies, honey?" said Mr. Hoffman.

"No," said the young lady flatly. "I like Walter Windshield because he talks so fast and funny."

This was quite a stopper for a pair of professionals like Mr. Hoffman and me. And possibly for Mr. "Walter Windshield" too, if he hears about it.

Figuring the juvenile mind is like trying to understand the atom bomb.

Kids like Lone Ranger. Lone Ranger rides a horse. What is better than horses? Ponies. You give away ponies.

What do children like? They like you because you talk so fast and funny. This is very discouraging. It is more than that. It is weird.

How are we to write television for the eight-year-old mind? When it hops about like a grasshopper.

"What is she laughing about now?" said Mr. Hoffman. The child was chortling at the screen where a young lady was eating a turkey leg.

"SWITCH IT ON!" I yelled at the earphones.

The sound came on with a bang. She likes it loud.

"I do not love you," sobbed the flickering screen. "Never, never, never."

"Shut it off," I said.

"So funny!" said the eight-year-old mind. "Eating a turkey leg!"

This week Miss Sarah Bernhardt has been sharing my meager lodgings. Miss Bernhardt is divine, as always. I am a great audience because Miss Bernhardt often addresses me as "Father." This is simply killing to both of us.

Miss Bernhardt, of course, is Miss Bernhardt pro tem. It is a passing phase, but very important. Miss Bernhardt appears in a school production called *Jack and the Beanstalk.*

Your tax-ridden correspondent witnesses here and now that this costs plenty of jack. Not deductible.

And I will begin by saying that when an eight-year-old lady takes up acting, she is apt to act all the time. Most of the time she acts as though her creaking parent is made of $5 bills.

Young lady actresses must never appear in public without being gussied to the eyebrows with new gloves and whatnot. None of which stores are giving away for free these days.

Also young ladies who are acting lose said gloves very frequently. About once a day I should imagine. That's an actress for you. Nothing but temperament.

Came the big day the other day and a good many parents settled themselves in comfortable seats to determine what all the past weeks' fuss was about.

There was a handy program guide for everybody, for

it turned out you could not tell the players without a program indeed. The entire lower grade was involved. It was
something like *Who's Who* where, as soon as you are listed,
you must buy. This assures a packed house. And by count, I
should judge about 100 small girls took part in *Jack and the
Beanstalk*.

This, if you are acquainted with little girls, is a powerful
amount of temperament.

The odd hundred ladies were sandwiched into the plot as
handfuls of Villagers, Spirits of Magic Beans, Little Mice,
Raindrops, Snowflakes, the Rainbow, Clouds and Helpers.

The play followed a conventional pattern.

A bill collector named Rafe Heywood is getting very pressing with Jack's mother before she can get down for a
touch at the Morris Plan. The mother sells the cow for some
quick scratch to put on a fast one at Santa Anita.

A blue sky artist talks Jack into selling the milk factory
first for a handful of beans. While everybody is hollering
murder, the beans grow up into a giant's house. Jack climbs
in and does a Raffles with the hen, the harp and the money-
bags.

The collector is paid off. Jack's mama has enough to bet
the 16-to-1 shots as long as she lives.

It is a live plot, as you well know.

Naturally, I kept a sharp eye out for my own Miss Sarah
Bernhardt in her first appearance upon the boards. With the
temperament of recent days, I figured she would certainly
blow her lines or do a Camille, crying "Armand, Armand."

But as it turned out, she came in a chorus line, listed
briefly as "The Giant's Evil Thoughts." Dressed in fetching
lipstick red and pretty much like any other little girl.

Didn't say a line. Didn't even carry a spear.

And when I think of the lost gloves and lost tempers which I have put up with, the Giant's evil thoughts were running out of the money alongside mine.

I suppose money is a problem to most people. But it is a perplexing matter to me. I am constantly searching the slick-cover magazines for ways to beat the system.

Once I found a budget in a large women's magazine. I followed it faithfully.

I allowed a fourth of the take for rent. A percentage for clothing. I put in 5 per cent for medical supplies. And allowed a cunning piece for schnapps in the event of melancholy.

I invested in insurance and laid out a cardboard inner sole for a rainy day. I started a Christmas fund. I divided my possessions equally between banker and butcher.

On paper, I was solvent, fluid. Heeled.

I sat back to enjoy life, free of money cares.

A month later, the snowstorm broke. The butcher was giving me a hurt look. And I was hocking my watch weekends to reach payday.

How it happened is a complete mystery to me. Even today.

I switched magazine subscriptions and soon was started on the baking powder can or teacup method.

"Get a series of baking powder cans," said the magazine article. "Label one 'Rent.' Another 'Food.' And so on."

The idea was to put the actual bullets in the guns. When the plumber called, you handed down the can labeled HOUSE REPAIR.

It took me a long time to save up baking powder cans. I

ate biscuits for weeks. With honey, with gravy, with butter and in shortcake.

I forgot to get a can labeled BRAWL FOR OLD FRIEND JUST BACK FROM KOREA.

The can labeled MISCELLANEOUS took a terrible beating. There *never* was enough money in MISCELLANEOUS. Consequently, I took in several movies on MEDICAL.

My tooth was fixed by GARDENING.

The gardener took a very stuffy attitude and was placated out of CLOTHING.

Everybody began to look very shabby. But nothing compared to the shabby looks I was getting from the department store which was holding a large marker.

In other words, the whole system went up the chimney.

I am closely in touch with Nature. And if you wish to observe Nature the best time is early in the morning when the dew sparkles on the grass and all the world is alive.

All except me. I am half dead at such hours. But no matter, I am up and walking around like a zombie.

The way to arrange this early rising with the blood coursing feebly in your veins, is to purchase a budgie. A budgie is an Australian bird. It is a small bird with a loud voice.

All day it sits silent. It rouses at dawn and lets go the loudest chirps I have ever heard. Our budgie can outshout a crow.

For a long time I thought our budgie was concealing one of those things in his mouth. You know the things you send 10 cents for. "Fool your friends. Throw your voice—under the bed, into a trunk. Have fun at parties."

It always seemed to me there was no point in purchasing furred and feathered friends. Because we have so many who come uninvited.

For a long time we had a family of raccoons. They came around midnight and threw the garbage can lid down the hill. BANG! BANG!

This brings a man out of a sound sleep with a reaction like insulin shock. I would put the flashlight on the garbage can and the whole raccoon family would stick their heads out and look at me.

They knew they were safe, for the law forbids taking a shotgun to them. They would look at me with a masked sneer.

Spare dogs visit my home. We have lots of dogs to spare around my house. My dog I could spare almost anytime.

He is always bringing an out-of-town friend home for dinner. When the friend reaches for the dinner—WOW! He beats the hide off him. You have never heard anything until you audition Mike and his friends having one dinner in a small kitchen.

Cats drop by and go hissing up the madrone trees. Dogs love to stand under trees and bark at cats after dinner. Just like gentlemen like to sit around and have a cigar. They like to bark all night. It is good for the digestion. Like a walk around the block.

Small children like to encourage dogs to bark like this. We have spare small children to go with each spare dog. It is a well-organized community.

The budgie pays no attention to all this racket. He is an early-morning worker and feels his best job is done when it is perfectly still.

There was some hint when I purchased this bird that he would talk.

"Budgies learn to talk if they are encouraged," said the book.

I have encouraged this budgie a good deal. Once I put a little champagne in his water cup. He should have a ball for himself and cut up a few touches with me on the World Series.

He got something that sounded like hiccups. But he never commented on a single batting average.

I have approached him on various subjects.

"Do you like Ike?"

He just looks at me. Did you ever have a budgie just stare at you? Not a wink. It's uncanny.

But at 5 o'clock in the morning! This bird is up and chatty as a bridge luncheon. Not a word of it worth repeating. *Chirp! Chirp! Tweet!*

This encourages the dog to rise and bark. And small children to run bright-eyed down the stairs and inquire:

"Did he say something? Did he talk?"

"Listen, cobber," I tell the bird. "How'd you like to be dropped in the East River in a cement overcoat?"

That bird hasn't given me a square answer yet. But one of these days we are going to have a quiet little chat. And then—

Possibly you remember the song as sung by Leadbelly and other graduates of the Big House school of music:

> *I'll never marry a farmer, he's always in the rain,*
> *I wanta marry the gambling man who wears the big gold*
> *chain . . .*

43

Well, I bring this up only as concerns my domestic life, which is a chancy matter in any case. And more so recently when Mr. Wilbur Clark sent me small roulette and dice tables.

Mr. Clark runs the Desert Inn at Las Vegas. The tables are two-foot miniatures. With green cloth and spinning wheel and various numbers. The dice table is also complete in detail—the same detail that has so genially swallowed my chancy scratch.

Well, I do not have to tell you what a dollhouse impression this made upon the cupcake who shares my Crackerjack prizes.

"Can I play?" she said breathlessly.

"As you know, my dear," I said, "your father has warned you against the evils of gaming. However, one must learn for oneself. So if you care to buck the tiger with a dime or so, I am your boy."

And in no time at all, this child had cunningly shaken down her piggy and socked it on the roulette table. Being a rank amateur, she popped it on Number 23.

"Now," I said spinning the wheel, "I am doing this all for a good purpose. So that you may see the futility of gambling."

"The ball has stopped on 23. I win," she cried.

"So it has," I said mopping my forehead. "But first spins do not count. I would not bet on numbers anyway. For you are sure to lose. Wouldn't you rather bet on red?"

"All right," she said.

The ball came up red.

"Your winning is temporary," I said. "This is the cruel thing about gaming. That you are led to invest your meager earnings in a sham."

Well, I do not care to recall the uncanny way this moppet was picking them. Black, red. Odd, even. Zero or double zero. If we had been in Las Vegas, Mr. Wilbur Clark would now be working for me.

The loss was fantastic. Even in dimes. As it approached $5 I was seriously thinking of wiring the wheel. A nefarious practice, but things were getting desperate.

The child was popeyed.

"Look at all the money I won!"

Ah, but then luck changed. And the dimes began to drift my way.

And like any gambler, the young lady poured more and more fever on the flames.

Finally when she was reduced to zero, she hustled upstairs and dug up two hidden dollars.

I cannot remember how many times I have tried to wheedle a small loan from her and been met with a firm denial that she has a single biscuit.

It took two spins and I was two dollars richer.

"So now you see what happens," I said. "And I trust this will be a lesson to you. Also a lesson not to hold out on your fond parent when he is trying to borrow a couple of quid for the show."

"You are not going to keep it?" she said.

"Why certainly," I said. "Else where is the lesson in all this?"

At this point, the little welsher put on one of the most terrible demonstrations I have ever witnessed.

"WAAAAAHHHH! It's my Christmas money and you took it!"

"Hush," I said, "what will the neighbors think?"

"I DON'T CARE! I WANT MY MONEY! WAAAHHH!"

So what can you do with somebody yelling copper on you like that? I cannot stand tears. So I returned the money. And I think in the count somehow got shaken for an extra dollar.

Totted up the accounts in my checkbook this morning and it seems I am on the shorts again. So I must go down to the village jug to make a touch.

I found the banker in a gloomy mood.

"Money is tight," said the banker. "We would probably require a financial statement."

"Be of good cheer, banker," I said. "I will make a financial statement. I will state that my income is low but my hopes are high. And now, if you will hand over the loot, man, I will give you my marker and all's well that ends well."

"It is not so easy as that," said the banker fingering the nuggets on his watch chain. "It is a matter of discount rates and the Federal Reserve Board. And such things I will not bore you with.

"The point seems to be," said the banker, "that sometimes we force money upon you. And at others you must cry every dime out of us. This," said the banker, "is one of those times."

Well, it seems I have been reading some such matters in the journals lately. Though it all seemed so complicated I could not see how it could possibly apply to me.

My own situation seemed fairly clear and outside such national statistics.

"My wants are simple, banker," I said. "Namely 500 skins, jawbone for one year."

"We must look at the broad picture," sighed the banker, closing the door and foreclosing a mortgage.

Now I have been looking at the broad picture of banking for many a co-signed year. I find it mighty strange.

In my early days of toiling on the journals, I was advised that my clear duty was to die for the city editor. And at times it appeared that I would do so. By starvation.

I staved off this prospect with loans from the bank.

In those days, I would approach the piggy on my knees crying, "Alms, for the love of Allah." The jug man would assume a serious expression and look over my application which held the co-signatures of two other lean and hungry journalists.

He would then give me a C-note and advise me to make my payments regularly.

Well, time passed and, with a few payroll adjustments (which the editor swore would ruin him), I shook loose from this annual drain.

I approached the banks only with deposits. I looked the banker squarely in the eye.

Did this improve my standing in the community? It ruined it, man.

"Banker," I said. "When I approached you for the ready some years ago, you were reluctant. For the simple reason that I had *not* been borrowing.

"This seemed a curious way of looking at it. To be reluctant when I did and reluctant when I did not. However," I said, "I am an agreeable individual. And your books will show you that I have kept coming and going in the highest traditions of the trust and savings dodge."

"True," said the banker. "But that was when we wished to loan you money. Nowadays it is better if you did not wish money. Then we might get around to pushing it on you again.

"That is the way money goes," said the banker gaily. "When you don't want it, you had better take it. And when you do want it, you had better not ask."

"Suppose I just hint a little?"

"That is better," said the banker. "Don't you call us. We'll call you."

2.

A HAPPY Thanksgiving wherever you may be. Mine is happy. But I am having a hard time explaining it to my guests. My guests are ten years old. They are filled with education and girlish laughter.

Was a time when these small fry about my groaning board were little ladies.

They accepted my tales with charming attention. Sometimes I chose to insert myself and a few Indians into the story of the Massachusetts Bay Colony. And I was not greeted with unladylike cries of: "Oh, what a fib, Mr. Delaplane!"

Alas, now we are ten and full of wisdom.

It was a great mistake to give ladies the vote. But it was worse when we taught them to read.

"Well, children, once upon a time there were a lot of people called Pilgrims and—"

"They had a Thanksgiving Day and ate turkey. We read about it in school."

"Are you trying to step on my lines?" I say sternly. "Pay attention. Your parent and host has some exclusive and unpublished data on the event.

"As I was saying, there were a lot of Pilgrims. Their names were Faith, Hope and Charity."

"All of them?"

"The three best ones," I say. "Three charming little girls who never, never interrupted. They were very thankful."

"What were they thankful for?"

"They were thankful because it was Thanksgiving. Mainly their father was thankful. He was thankful because there was no TV. There was no TV urging him to smell sweeter or get richer or smoke filtered cigarettes.

"Oh, it was a wonderful life. There were no cowboys galloping and hollering while he was trying to read the evening paper. Nobody advised him how to brush his teeth or to eat crackling breakfast food.

"He was also thankful because there were no telephones. So he did not have to fall over the cat in the middle of the night to advise people that they had the wrong number."

"But why were the little Pilgrim girls thankful?" they said. "Without TV, too."

"They were thankful because their father was thankful," I said. "As all little girls should be.

"Now one day, their father said to them: 'Faith, Hope and Charity, I have in mind to hold a big Thanksgiving Day celebration. What would you like for dinner?'"

"Turkey!" says my well-educated audience.

"Turkey," I agree. "So the Pilgrim father took down his musket and filled it up with bullets and he went out in the woods. Almost immediately a lot of Indians shot him full of arrows."

"Did it hurt?"

"It hurt him terribly. But he was so brave he didn't even cry. He was about as brave as I am," I say reminiscently. "Why, I remember the Custer and the Sioux—"

"Were you there?"

Well, when these ladies were six years old, I was careless in some of these stories. But no more.

"My grandfather was there. He told me," I say. That holds them.

"Well, he shot the Indians who shot him. And what do you know? One of the Indians was on his way home from the Supermarket. And he had a big bag with a broad-breasted turkey. All white meat. So the Pilgrim father took it home and Faith, Hope and Charity had it for dinner."

"Who got the long end of the wishbone?"

"Faith," I said. "Because she was youngest.

"They cooked up the turkey as follows: Five ounces of maple syrup, six ounces of butter, a teaspoon of cinnamon, a half teaspoon of cloves, two quarts of cider, a half pint of Demarara rum and a pint of New England rum. Heat syrup, butter and spices until it bubbles. Add cider and simmer. Add rum, stir and mull with a red-hot poker."

"For turkey?" they said.

"Well, no," I said. "It appears that I have picked up a recipe for hot buttered rum by mistake. But if you young ladies will retire to the television, your father has a scientific experiment in the kitchen."

Having got myself nicely settled in the suburbs, I read with interest there is a great movement back to the city.

"Suburban statistics show a definite trend toward town,"

says the story. "Even with modern improvements, many people seem to find living more comfortable in urban dwellings."

You ain't just a-whistlin' "Dixie," Professor.

The urge to the country came about with a great rash of country books. *We Went Back to the Land.* That kind of thing.

I know it certainly sounded good to me.

There was this couple, see? And, man, he was cracking his back in the insurance business, see? So they went back to the land. Land's sake, what a life.

The way I read this, they got up early in the morning.

They tossed a few handfuls of corn to the chickens. The chickens were delighted as a Congressman meeting a voter. They ate the corn. Meanwhile, back at the chicken house, this sneaky couple were dipping the nests for chicken eggs.

What they didn't eat, they sold. Bought applejack with the money probably. They didn't say.

This certainly sounded like the life to me. I would go out and get a bunch of chickens and set them to work for me.

Let me tell you it did not work out thataway.

In the first place, the suburbs are one of the snootiest places you can possibly live. You can raise chickens in a city apartment sooner than in the suburbs. The suburban people pass laws against it.

I hear now they are passing laws in our county against keeping burros.

It seems that Sears Roebuck will sell you a burro for $50.

It was my intention to buy a couple of these beasts. I would feed them hay or burro seed. Or whatever burros eat. And I would rent them out for rides to neighborhood moppets.

Not so. No sooner do burros come on the market at a reasonable price but they pass laws against them.

For some time I thought about raising turkeys. You get desperate when you have been shoveling coal for the dailies all these years.

There is no law against turkeys. Only chickens.

I would raise turkeys and get rich.

Do you know it is almost impossible to raise a turkey? True. Turkeys are the most delicate birds alive. They stay alive only with the help of specialists standing around their bed. Day and night nurses.

It seems turkeys have no sense to come in out of the rain. When it rains they get their feet wet. When they get their feet wet, they die.

They do not come in and dry off. Or take aspirin and fruit juices. They just pop off in the most ungrateful way.

There is not a thing on my shady acres that brings in a crying dime. For a time I thought of taking out some of the redwoods. We would chop a redwood and sell the wood for cheery fires.

Well, it happens we *had* to take out a redwood recently. The cost of taking out a redwood is about the same as taking out an appendix.

My child opened a lemonade stand. Unfortunately, we are on a dead-end street. Nobody comes up the street but the postman and people who make the wrong turn. I wound up having to buy the lemonade myself. Delicious but expensive.

One of the curiosities of our times is the curiosity of industry. It is not enough for industry to sell you a bed. They must know why you sleep in a bed.

Scarcely a day goes by but industry is out snooping around the customer.

"Making a survey," says the gentleman at the door. "Will you kindly enlighten us why you sleep in a bed?"

"Because the floor is so hard," you answer.

This information is taken down along with the answers of millions of other people who sleep in beds. The whole thing is fed into a machine.

A few weeks later, the statistical men come out with all sorts of vital information: More people sleep in beds than on fire escapes. The average bed sleeper turns over 143 times during the night. Whereas the fire-escape sleeper turns over only once—after one turn they pick him up off the sidewalk.

Well, what I started to say: I have just read a survey on refrigerators. The refrigerator people sent out their surveyors, they should peek in people's iceboxes.

They found vitamin pills and beauty creams. Damp clothes waiting to be ironed, and angora sweaters. A lady kept her shoes in the refrigerator—claimed it made them easier to get on in hot weather.

It is not often that surveyors come up with new information like this. And it is obvious that the whole refrigerator must be redesigned. It must be designed to hold all the perishable extras that milady creams on her face. Compartments must be added for the wet wash. There should be a chilling department for shoes.

Surely times have changed since the iceboxes I recall. If I had put shoes in the icebox, my grandma would have lathered me up considerably.

Nobody came around and surveyed us. But I imagine our icebox was standard.

Our icebox contained mainly ice. About 50 pounds when it was loaded. And 50 pounds of ice leaves room for very little except the milk and the leftover roast.

Our ice was delivered Tuesday and Friday. It was delivered by a husky iceman in a blue suit with a leather apron over one shoulder. It was delivered in a wooden wagon drawn by a horse in a straw hat. The straw hat had holes cut in it so the horse's ears came through.

The iceman would climb up on a little step and chop off 50 pounds with his pick. He took a pair of tongs and hoisted this on his back and took it in the house and put it in the box.

While he was gone, all of us small fry climbed in the back of the cool wagon and sucked little chunks of chopped ice. When the iceman came back, we jumped out and ran.

It was legend on our block that the iceman had once chopped up a small boy in the dark. Accidentally mistaking him for a piece of ice. We did not get this out of a survey. It was general talk, which is much more satisfactory.

Now, of course, everything is changed. All my ice is made overnight by electric elves. It comes in little plastic trays.

I must say I had never considered it as a storage spot for the laundry. Or for shoes. The modern refrigerator has all sorts of possibilities I never knew. Until the refrigerator people surveyed them.

It seems to me this simply adds to the confusion of our days. Confusion and expense. For if you do a late snack in the icebox and accidentally chew up madam's new I. Millers, it is a lot more expensive than cold steak.

We seem to be in a season of emergencies. My heiress has put her knee through the glass door. A matter of nine silver bullets to the glazier for repairs.

Last week she put her hand through a window. Another $9. Plus 16 stitches and hysterics that set all the neighborhood dogs to howling. In sympathy, I suppose.

"Couldn't you just stay away from everything made of glass?" I asked, gloomily. "Your antique parent does not own a single share of Owens-Illinois. More's the pity."

"It was an accident," she said. "Don't you understand? I just pushed the window and it broke. You aren't sympathetic."

Well, I am sympathetic. Just slightly worn out around the wallet, that's all.

Just about the time I get the household budgeted, the wind blows the shingles off the roof.

The dog develops an asthma that can only be cured by injections of liquid gold and a diet of fresh caviar.

This dog has the appetite of a starving tiger. Yet I have never seen a more delicate animal. The only dog in the world who gets poison oak. The only dog I have ever seen who scratches with both hind feet at once.

The dog is on a budget of horse meat. Which at present prices is about the same as filet mignon. Just to stagger around the house, he requires gallons of this expensive fodder.

He tears into everything that is left over as though he expected food to go out of style.

Thereafter he lies whimpering on the best rug. Regarding me with brimming eyes and the wistful look of a child with a nose pressed against the candy window.

"I'm hungry," he says. "*Starving!*"

Once I figured out the amount of horse meat this dog has

eaten. I figured he has eaten ten full-grown horses during his lifetime!

With what this dog has eaten I could have bought Nashua.

Rushing a gory child to the doctor in the middle of the night is bad enough. It is the aftermath of patient suffering and smug bravery that is so annoying.

For days now I have had to listen to every detail. How she bled fiercely, meanwhile making sad and courageous last statements. Advising her father not to sorrow too greatly, but to regard the whole episode as an angel snatched from his bosom.

I have had a background of constant telephone conversations to other young ladies.

"Cut so bad they had to stick my hand back on!

"Blood over *everything*! It was terrible!

"My father said he had *never* seen anyone so brave! I hardly cried a bit."

So short is memory. I wouldn't call it crying. More like bellowing. Like a cow with colic. More like a roar, I would say.

As to Father and what he has seen, I grow quite faint at the sight of blood. I don't know how we got the emergency bandage on. Neither of us could bear to look, and that's a fact.

I keep a first-aid package and a first-aid book around the house. But when the emergency arises I can never find the right page. I am just as likely to give artificial respiration as anything else.

Only one thing I have learned to do until the doctor

comes. Give them first aid and give them lemonade. There is nothing like lemonade for shock, no matter what the books say. I know. I drank a quart of it myself.

When the Wright brothers were still wondering what kept those things up in the air, I was wondering, too. I remember making some pretty tricky experiments.

You take some theme paper. And you fold it in the middle. Then you fold— Well, this is probably too technical.

What I am getting at is the difference between me and the rest of the aeronautical experts. I am still wondering.

I suppose I am as unlikely a person as any to induct youth into the upper air. Yet parents are called upon for many things. So the other day I must take my ten-year-old daughter on her first flight to New York.

"I'm scared," she said quite frankly.

Well, frankly, I am slightly nervous, too. Up in the wild, blue yonder. Will it go up? Will it stay up? It always does. But I see no more reason for it than when I sailed papers in the classroom.

"There is absolutely nothing to be afraid of," I said firmly. "Ten thousand people are flying in airplanes every day between four and five in the afternoon.

"You are braver than me," she said. "Anyway you have more experience."

Well, that is me, children. What an actor! The Iroquois chief at the stake. Smiling disdainfully through the flames as the howling squaws slice pork chops off me.

Out on the hardstand at the airport, the big red and silver Constellation stood waiting with open doors.

To tell the truth, I had visions of dragging the moppet

screaming into the big silver bird. She was shuttled like cargo on airplanes when she was at the bubbling age. But she has forgotten, of course.

"I sincerely hope you will make no scene," I said gloomily. "For possibly the other passengers would think you inherited your craven attitude from your intrepid parent."

"I'm not scared any more," she said. "I think you're scared of airplanes."

"Who, me?" I cried. "Why, sometime I must tell you of my early classroom experiments. Wilbur and Orville came to me, frankly at wit's end and—"

"I don't believe a word of it," she said.

The younger generation not only flies so calmly I am enraged. There is also little respect for aeronautical pioneers, it seems to me.

The big silver bird took off like a big silver bird. (Which they always do, to my amazement.)

The lady in the blue uniform said she welcomed us aboard. She gave us chewing gum and said would we kindly belt ourselves to the seats and refrain from smoking.

The small fry gave my arm one clutch as we roared down the runway. Then as we lifted into the air, she grew a great big smile.

"There isn't anything to it, is there?" she said.

"Just as I told you," I said.

A surprised look came on her face. She prodded her mouth with her tongue.

"Anything wrong?" I said.

"I swallowed my gum," she said.

I wear a peculiar wristwatch. And when I woke and looked

at it this morning, it certainly was a surprise. The inside was quite moist. Clouded like a car window on a brisk day.

The reason I am surprised is because this watch could spend 20 years at the bottom of the Aegean Sea. When a pearl fisherman hauls it up, it runs as if it had spent the whole time in the window of Cartier's.

That is what it says in the advertisements for my watch.

My watch spends time on top of K-2. It dives in submarines. It falls off the dock at Puerto Barrios. It is absolutely foolproof.

How does water get into my watch, confounding the experts? Confound it, I will tell you.

I keep a good many things at my bedside. For I am the executive type. Everything at hand.

I keep my watch, my notebook, magazines, chewing gum, cigarettes, mystery stories, newspapers, old manuscripts, unanswered mail, paper, pencils and French novels. I could wake at any moment of the night and hang out a shingle and go into business.

As a matter of fact, I often do go into business. For I am often visited by a transient young lady from the next room.

"Can I borrow a pencil? Mine is broken."

"Will you return it? Cross your heart and hope to die?"

So far nothing has ever been returned. Though I often find the pencils under the couch. They are well chewed. She has excellent teeth.

Well, you can hardly blame youth for being impressed with my collection of executive material.

I have a box with paper clips. You cannot make toy airplanes without paper clips. I have airmail stickers and stationery stolen from the better hotels.

I have a small wheel that tells you what time it is in any part of the world. I am a treasure chest. A bedded-down Five & Ten Cent Store.

I am an oasis in the night. For I have an unlimited supply of water. True, I must rise frequently and refill the glass. But that is no matter.

"Can I have a drink of your water?"

"My dear," I cry, "why not bring a glass of water to your own beside? Like your executive-type parent? It is a small matter of turning the tap and—"

"Yours tastes better," she says honestly. "Besides, I forgot."

"Don't turn on the light then. And please, please, don't spill it."

"I won't."

CRASH!

"I'm sorry."

I have had long, quiet talks with this child. I have tried the knout and the rack and the Iron Maiden. I have withdrawn allowances.

"You are being terribly destructive. I cannot possibly fix your bicycle when you bend the handle bars."

I honestly believe this frail child could tear telephone books in half. And bend horseshoes. Things she brings home bent have to be straightened by a blacksmith.

Well, it appears that she did not bend the handle bars. It was a horrid girl at school. This girl, I gather, is something like Frankenstein's monster.

"She took the bike and *threw* it down. Just *threw* it down. And I was very polite. Just like you told me. And I said 'Please, don't throw the bike down.' But she just *threw* it down."

Anyway, what I was saying about my watch? My watch is completely waterproof. It spends days hanging in a goldfish bowl in the jeweler's window.

It was engineered by men of science. Each turned screw is cunningly fitted. It runs dryly automatic.

Which is why I cannot understand how a small girl,

hardly in long division, can fling water into it with one careless hand. And in the dark at that.

I woke up this morning to hear the budgie break off his
twittering and announce: "Hand me that wrench, Joe."

"A cage break!" I gasped. "Kick on the siren. Turn on the
searchlights. I knew that bird could talk."

At this point, a strange man stuck his head in the bed-
room door.

"I can't find no leak," he said briskly. He pulled his head
back out of sight.

"The plumber is here," announced my offspring. She likes
to see the house torn apart. It lends excitement to the day.

The plumbing people were downstairs with their ears
pressed against the wall.

"I don't even *hear* it leaking," he said accusingly.

"It leaks for me," I said miserably. "Puddles. Gallons."

This is the problem with a household leak. For me it pours
like a hose. When the plumbers arrive, it sulks.

The leak started boldly enough. My house had just been
finished. The builder went around turning things on and off
to test them. He filled the bathtub with water and then
pulled the plug. There was a great spattering noise downstairs.

We went down and found the living room filled with water.

"That's funny," he said.

"Crazy, man," I said. "Possibly this is very modern. The
water runs out the front door and waters the garden."

"I don't think so," he said thoughtfully. "Why not have it
run directly into the garden then?"

"So what makes sense in a modern house?"

The builder climbed up into a little 'tween-decks attic. "The pipes aren't hooked up," he said.

Well, we hooked up the pipes and the water ran through them. A week or so later I was taking a shower and auditioning myself on "Flatfoot Floogie with the Floy, Floy."

"The water's coming through the ceiling!" screamed my heiress.

"Nonsense," I said, switching to "Nobody Rambled like My Rambling Rose." "Kindly do not interrupt when I am taking my singing lessons."

"Can I put on my g'loshes and wade in it?"

It was pretty wet all right. I called the plumber. He said he would be right over.

At noon, the plumber's office called. Would somebody be home all afternoon? They wanted to be sure they could get in. Somebody was in all afternoon. But not the plumber.

Plumbers arrive at 6 o'clock in the morning. I do not know why. I suspect all plumbers are out night-clubbing. They come by on their way home.

By this time the water had dried up. I turned on the shower again.

"It pours out of here like a faucet," I said. "Watch."

We watched for half an hour. Nothing.

I went upstairs and took a shower. I sang in the shower and danced in the shower. Nothing.

The plumber said something vague about the leak sealing itself off.

When he went away, I turned on the water again, Splash! Spatter, spatter, spatter. I rushed to the telephone.

"It's leaking again," I said.

The plumber was back within a half hour. The leak had stopped.

"You can see the water on the floor," I said desperately.

"Maybe you spilled some accidentally. Maybe the bird spilled it."

This has been going on for nearly a month. We have tried all sorts of devices. The plumber sneaks up on it. We have ripped up the flooring. Checked the pipes. Dry as the dust bowl.

But let me start a shower with no plumber around and *whoosh!* It's real crazy, man, crazy. Or else I am.

I read in the journals that a young boy is high on the honors list of China. This boy denounced 281 people to the secret police in one year. Including his papa.

This is a fair score. But I will stack my own heiress in this league any day.

This child denounces me daily. She denounces me and other people and, if I did not shut her off, would still be denouncing far into the night. I think this child could denounce 281 people in a day. And have spares left for an encore.

"I can't do this old homework and I hate *everybody!*"

Well, when we get secret police in America I expect I will be first to go. Brain-washed, confessed and heartily ashamed of myself.

It may be slim pickings for these little denouncers the second year. But the first year will be a real slaughter.

Somehow I thought when I left the ivied halls of education, I was through with homework. Any more would be double jeopardy. It turns out such is not the case.

There I was reading the paper of an evening. Disagreeing with the editorials and laughing like crazy over the comics.

"What do you know about Shasta Dam?"

"Don't your books say?" I asked sternly. "After all, you are being educated. It would not be fair for me to tell you."

"The books don't say," she said tragically. "I looked and looked."

"How do the other children find out?"

"Their fathers tell them, I guess."

"This seems highly unlikely to me. However, what is the question?"

"Well, we have to write something on Shasta Dam and I don't know why and I don't know anything about it."

"How much do you have to write?"

"Two paragraphs. But I don't know *anything*."

"My dear," I said, "Shasta Dam is a family curse. At one time when your father was toiling on rewrite—I recall that it was a warm Saturday morning when expert reporters are off and medium-priced slobs do the work.

"It was on this fateful day that a gentleman by name of Mr. Harold Ickes did something very important about Shasta Dam and something called the Raker Act.

"What he did," I said, "I never rightly understood. But the editor handed it to me and suggested that I whip it into many paragraphs of elegant prose."

"What about my homework?"

"Homework will wait. This is a lesson in patience and guile. Anyway, I went to the newspaper library and looked up Shasta Dam. It seemed this thing had been going on for years and the assorted clips filled two shoe boxes."

"We just have to write two paragraphs, that's all."

"You could not begin to tell the story of Shasta Dam in

two paragraphs. It involves costs and water flow and power companies and politics. I point out to you that I had one hour to get this into the newspaper."

"I want my homework! I don't know about Shasta Dam!"

"Nor did I," I said. "Except that it is full of water. Which is good for washing and brushing your teeth and things like that. However, by looking carefully in the clippings, I found a scholarly piece done by a high-priced reporter.

"I removed this piece, rewrote the beginning and copied the rest. It was well received and, while they did not raise my pay, it looked well on my report card."

"But what shall I do?"

"I have just outlined the method," I said. "Get out the encyclopedia. Rewrite the first paragraph and copy the second."

I must report that I was roundly denounced as a card sharp and a poor parent. But what is a poor parent to do? I swore off homework years ago. I have no intention of backsliding.

The yellow jackets have been fierce this year. They live up in the oaks and madrone trees, up on the hill. But they use the house for board of directors' luncheons.

They are irritable beggars and are likely to sting. I understand after they sting you, they go off and die. This is not much consolation though. A lady name of Elizabeth Opfinger did some experiments with bees. She proved they were fairly dumb and did not recognize the color of a flower when blowing the safe for honey.

However, my bees recognize me immediately. They have me figured for a bombing run.

The other day I built a bee trap. It was sent to me in the

mail and is as good as anything Mr. Rube Goldberg ever thought up. Lady said it was sure-fire.

Take a funnel and stuff the funnel tube with hamburger. Plug the small end with a cork.
Now take the funnel and turn it upside down and hang it over a big bowl of strong detergent.

The idea is this: The yellow jackets fly up under the big end of the funnel and begin to work on the hamburger. When they fly out, they lose their sense of direction or something. Anyway, they fly into the detergent.

This serves them right for flying by the seat of their pants instead of on instruments.

The news that I was making a bee trap spread around the neighborhood. And while the neighbors paid little attention, having no faith in my projects, a good many small fry were on hand.

The lady who sent me the bee trap failed to give me one specification. I will give it to you: Load your bee trap inside.

The yellow jackets could hardly wait for me to bait the trap. They were that anxious to eat the hamburger and go splash.

"The idea of the bee trap is to catch bees," I told my audience.

"Like the one on your arm?"

"Where?" I said. "Take him off."

"My mother says let bees alone and they will let you alone."

"Your mother—" I said—"I withdraw that. Here, you hold the hamburger."

"Uh, uh," he said backing away.

"They won't hurt you," I said. *"Ouch!"*

Well, the upshot was I dropped the hamburger and we all retreated. It was a terrific trap. But I couldn't get close enough to set it. Yellow jackets were buzzing up and down the hill with the good news and more were showing up all the time.

I went in the house and consulted an article by Mr. Ronald Ribbands, entomologist for the Rothamsted Experimental Station near London.

Of more than two million kinds of insects in the world, the bee is the one we know most about and the one most useful to us. We are apt to associate them first with honey and secondly, perhaps, with their sting.

Anyone who associates them secondly, perhaps, with their sting is of little value.

I went out and turned the hose on the hamburger.

We baited up the old bee trap and hung it up.

Works all right. Just like the lady said. The yellow jackets flew in. When they flew out they flew into the detergent. The only trouble was not many cared for the bee trap. Many of them preferred a small boy who had been eating raw hamburger when I wasn't watching. He still smelled good and was easier to get at.

This has caused a good deal of misinformation around the neighborhood. And the story seems to be that I get young children up to the house and feed them raw hamburger and let bees sting them.

"If a dog was called 'horse,' would he think he was a horse?"

"I beg your pardon?" It is rather startling the way these

questions pop out of unformed minds. Here I am polishing my boots, waiting for the Muse to strike fire. Thinking up tales of blood and slaughter.

"What I mean, if you had a dog, you know? And when he was young, a little bitty puppy, you called him a horse. Would he grow up and think he was a horse? That's what I mean."

"Is this a joke?" I asked suspiciously. Many times these things end with some of the corniest punch lines since Joe Miller.

"No, really and truly. Because if you called him 'horse,' how would he know he was a dog?"

"He could look at other dogs. Also horses. He could make comparisons. For one thing he would notice that he was not wearing a saddle."

"But if he never saw a horse or a dog."

"Could we postpone this, my dear? Your parent does not have all the answers. Never having raised a dog from a little bitty puppy calling him 'horse.' How would I know?"

"You should know. You're a grownup," she said sniffing.

Well, there is the problem. Sooner or later they discover your feet of clay. And while a good deal has been written about the suffering of persons who discover the plaster feet on their idols, mighty little has been said about the chagrin of the man with the clay feet.

It seems I can hardly turn around these days but what my reputation is fraying at the edges.

"If somebody walked up to you and pointed a pistol at you, you know? And they said, 'Say you are not a Christian or I will shoot you.' What would you do?"

"I would say, 'Shoot,'" I said bravely. "I would tell them, 'I have a daughter who asks so many questions I don't care whether I live or die.'"

"No, really."

"I would tell them I was a Mohammedan."

"You shouldn't do that. It is a denial of faith."

"Says who?"

"Our Sunday school teacher says so. She says you should never deny your faith no matter what."

"How many shots has your Sunday school teacher heard fired in anger? I suppose somebody has been around pointing a big old pistol at her lately."

"You don't understand. She says you must stand up for your faith and—"

"So," I said bitterly. "I am to stand around while somebody shoots me with a great big pistol. I don't notice the lady you quote going around asking people to shoot her. At least I haven't read anything about it in the newspapers. No, nor any beat-up cupcake either. But me, I have to go get shot full of holes."

"You don't understand," she said loftily. "My Sunday school teacher says."

It seems the world is just overrun with people egging on the young to get their father shot full of holes. If we are not personally punctured, our reputations are certainly ragged.

"I do so understand," I said. "And I am thinking seriously of becoming a Mohammedan. Like we read about in *Life* magazine. Then if anybody pointed a pistol at me, I would have a ready answer."

"You'd have to go to Africa," she said.

"And so I will," I said. "I will join the Foreign Legion. Boy, will you be sorry when I come back in my sharp uniform. Like in the movies—"

"Really!" she said. "If you called a dog 'horse,' what do you think?"

What is so rare as a day in April? Two blackberry vines over the creek are green with spring. The sun is warm and the boxer dog is rolling in the new clover.

"Blast and this and that," I cry. "GITOFFA THE NEW CLOVER!"

The dog goes off to check the rabbit action, across the creek. He gives me a huffy look.

I don't care. I am a horticulturist. I cannot be bothered with his feelings. Science is inflexible. Where is the trowel?

It appears the trowel is up the street somewhere. Why?

"I was fixing my bicycle with it, Daddy."

"My dear," I say kindly. "How can you fix a bicycle with a trowel?"

"You can't," she says. "I tried. But—well, you know the screw that comes down on that thing? Well it was coming off—"

"Never mind," I say. "Can you get it back?"

"When Anne comes home from school. She put it somewhere.

Well, no mind. Did my great-grandpa have a trowel when he broke the prairie soil of Illinois? No, sir. He had a plow. I have no plow but I am not helpless. I have ingenuity. Also a large spoon.

Well, you'd think I had taken the crown jewels. Heaven knows a little fresh spring dirt never hurt silver. Okay, I will use a kitchen spoon. Hey-ho.

Hey-ho. Hey-ho. What is spring without the Ferry seed catalogue? Eggs without ham.

I have lettuce seeds. Directions:

> Sow seed as early in Spring as ground can be worked.
> Spade ground well, and lay out rows about 18 inches apart.

It is very hard to spade ground with an 18-inch kitchen spoon. Did you know that?

"Would you like to help your father, my dear?"

"No."

"Come, come," I said sternly. "Is this the spirit of the pioneers? Don't you like lettuce?"

"I like lettuce from the store," she said frankly. "Anyway we never get lettuce. The raccoons always eat it."

What can you expect at that age? I am a hardy type. I think I will hitch up the wagons and move West. I will put the south 40 in cucumbers.

> Sow seed after danger of frost is past and the ground is warm. Rich, rather sandy soil is best.

My soil is rich as a mother's heart.

> Make the hills 4 to 6 feet apart; place 8 or 10 seeds in each hill; cover one inch deep.

This is the kind of gardening I like. One inch deep. My back gets a little stiff from spading with a kitchen spoon. But those are only unused muscles. I am all steel wire underneath. Sleepless and alert with the old Winchester when the redskins are on the prowl.

"Will you kindly remove the cat?" I could use a little cooperation it seems to me. The Siamese kitten has been following along. As I plant, she bats the dirt around. This uncovers the seeds.

I am informed that the cat will be removed. In a minute.

The dog comes back, panting from three fast rounds with a mythical rabbit. He flops down on the earth I have spaded so carefully with the spoon. I don't suppose it will hurt it though. It is a good thing I am built of coiled springs. An ordinary man would give up with a back like this.

I am planting lettuce and cucumbers. Onions and parsley and carrots. If the H-bomb comes I am prepared. The fact that it is a race between me and the raccoons is no matter at all.

For a good many years now I have been planting. And the raccoons have moved in and gobbled the product. This year I have chosen my crop with care. Everything in my garden goes well with raccoon roast.

Speaking of houses, the most interesting thing we did when building our house was to put in a brick stairway.

We are in the midst of adding a new room to the dwelling. The yard is full of lumber. And the children are stepping on the nails. It is the most delightful season of the year.

"Absolutely *no* brick stairway!"

That was the only thing I put my foot down on when we built.

In my gay and gory journalist days, I was often assigned to the emergency hospital. If you look down the blotter of the day's emergencies, you find a startling repetition:

"Falling down stairs. Contusions, possible skull fracture."

We built a house of reasonably soft wood. Wooden walls,

wooden roof (the kind that catches on fire easily when the chimney blows sparks). We built a wooden garage.

What did we build for stairs? Brick.

Not only that. When you tumble down these badly lit, hard, brick stairs, you land on a solid brick floor.

If I were building a booby trap, I would design such a house.

I worked out the statistics: "Of five people admitted to emergency hospital, four will have injuries resulting from household falls."

I pointed out that frame houses stand safely during earthquakes.

"Most persons injured in the San Francisco earthquake of '06 were hit by bricks from toppling chimneys."

I got out the blueprints. I showed how the stairway bricks hung like the sword of Damocles, right above the dining table.

I painted a purple word picture. The festive family is gathered around the festive board. Rumble! Rumble! Crash!

The neighbors come in. They pick you up with the thing you use to turn pancakes with.

Everybody listened. They said: "Gee, Daddy knows a lot, doesn't he?"

Then we went ahead and built a brick staircase.

It has kept us on our toes—for want of a better word.

One hilarious thing about this stairway—we will probably die laughing about it—is the telephone.

We have a long cord on the telephone. The telephone comes out of a closet. And the cord stretches right across the stairs. It is as effective as a trip wire in a mine field. It is well camouflaged—blends right in with the brick.

Catch this cord just right with your foot and you come down like a stage comic. It is really comical and we all enjoy it. (Our insurance rates are a little high. But we all agree it is worth it.)

3.

NOT everybody is lucky enough to get in on the birth of an organization. I will be glad to tell you about the Redwood Terrace Club and how it grew.

The present membership is three girls, generally in the eleven-year-old range. I am a sort of honorary member.

The dues are 10 cents a month. When the subject of dues came up at our meeting, everybody looked rather expectantly at me. I paid. The treasurer's report shows we are in sound financial shape. Debts: none. Cash on hand: 10 cents.

The purpose of this club is to hold meetings.

Another purpose of our club is to raise money by selling penny chocolate bars and a soft drink called "Kool-Aid." Since it would have upset the treasury to purchase the original supply, the funds were supplied by an honorary member, who wishes to remain anonymous. The club thanks him.

The Redwood Terrace Club meets at the foot of my driveway. People backing out should be careful not to run over the members.

The way it got its name was like this: We were poking around down the canyon and ran into four beautifully sawed redwood logs. Each was about two feet high.

It was perfectly obvious (to everybody but the honorary member, a rich but dull-witted fellow) that here was the making of a store. You simply set the logs on end, stretched a couple of planks between them and set out your merchandise.

The honorary member was dispatched forthwith to find two planks. When he returned, the store had grown into a club. Since he kept hanging around, there was nothing to do but vote him in.

The first meeting was called to order by the president before she was elected president. When it became obvious she was going to be elected, she put on a distressingly false show of modesty. However, she accepted the post.

The members then went downhill to the store to purchase the supplies. They were somewhat late returning, having found and adopted a lost kitten. The honorary member was appointed to de-flea the new cat.

The honorary member then rose and said: "Madam President. When the Redwood Terrace Club raises money from selling Kool-Aid, what will be done with the money?"

The members then went into executive session. When they came out, they informed the honorary member as follows:

"When we get a lot of money, about $5,000, we will give it to charity like maybe an orphanage."

The honorary member then revealed to the membership that he, himself, was an orphan and a worthy target of charity. He suggested that they give him the first $5.

The suggestion was howled down without being put to formal vote.

The honorary member then pointed out that the Kool-Aid stand was at the end of a one-block, dead-end street. That there were few likely customers except himself and other parents.

It was voted that the honorary member should construct street signs reading, THIS WAY TO THE REDWOOD TERRACE CLUB. KOOL-AID 10 CENTS. He was further advised to place these signs at regular intervals on all main intersections.

The honorary member then withdrew in a sulk and went in the house and began to read his old book, the meanie.

The Redwood Terrace Club opened its annual Kool-Aid sale at 6:30 P.M., the regular opening having been postponed by charity work for a lost kitten. Only two lost cars came up the dead-end street and no sales were made.

It then being time for dinner, the membership voted to let the honorary member purchase what was left. Which was about half, the rest having been drunk by the membership.

The honorary member agreed on condition he did not have to drink it. The membership voted to drink the remainder tomorrow and the meeting was adjourned.

The second meeting of the club was called to order with three charter members present. Also noted as present was the honorary member who happens to be me.

Present likewise were two dogs who like to hang around but have no vote.

The lady president then rose and declared that the club purpose has been changed.

"We should raise animals like in a zoo. like rats and snakes and guppies."

The honorary member then rose and said if the club was going to raise rats he begged to resign.

"Furthermore," said the honorary member, "I am not going to have a lot of rats raised on the property. Nor snakes either. I thought the purpose of this club was to see mushy pictures. And learn to walk wobbly like Marilyn Monroe. That was the purpose last time."

"We changed the purpose. Anyway, we don't mean rats like rats. We mean like the rats you get in pet stores. Oh, they're so cute! And they run up your arm and sit on your head and everything!"

The honorary member said firmly that no rat was going to run up *his* arm and sit on *his* head.

"Why don't you have a nice charity club? Doing good works?"

"What kind of good works?"

"Why, all sorts of good works. You could visit the sick and carry them calf's-foot jelly."

"Calf's-foot jelly! Ugh! How awful!"

"All the girls I read about carried calf's-foot jelly to the sick. Like Rebecca of Sunnybrook Farm. And a young lady I seem to remember as Freckles. And a ray of sunshine who was glad she had crutches."

"Why was she glad she had crutches?"

"Because she didn't have to use them."

"That's a silly reason."

"It does seem so," the honorary member admitted. Though when I read it as a youth, it seemed quite noble.

The members then asked the honorary member to withdraw while they held an executive session. The honorary member retired gloomily to the house for a short beer.

When he returned, he was informed that the purpose of the club was to raise money.

"That is a worth-while purpose. How will you raise this money?"

"We thought—well, maybe—well, we thought we could help you. You know like with your work. Like sharpening pencils."

"What is the current rate for sharpening pencils?"

"We need $2.35. We could sharpen that many."

"And what will be done with this club fund?"

"Well, that's what it costs for a pair of rats. Now I know you're going to say no. But we got it all figured out. It's so easy! And you'll never know they're around. We're going to build a little house for them! Real cute! Way out in back."

The honorary member then rose and begged to state that if anybody—*anybody* at all and that included his own daughter, maybe even particularly his own daughter—brought *any* rat near his house, the club, including all members, would not sit down for a week.

The honorary member then sat down. The membership then informed him that maybe they would move their club over to somebody else's driveway. Where the father was not *mean!*

The honorary member said they could do just that.

The meeting then broke up, all members declaring that *nobody* could have any fun any more and everything was a big *mess!*

The Redwood Terrace Club asked me to address the membership on Labor Day. The matter was stated very well by the president:

"Why don't they have Labor Day *during* the school year? So we could have a holiday."

The club members then took their places. And I, an honorary member, rose and spoke as follows:

"Madam President and ladies of the Redwood Terrace Club. It is indeed a singular honor to be invited here today and to look down upon your intelligent faces.

"It is my opinion that a good deal of malarkey about Labor is being sawed off on the young. Much is said about the dignity of Labor. But has anyone said anything about how dignified it is to sit around and do nothing?

"A person sitting around doing nothing has time to think about being dignified and put some work in it.

"The whole point of Cinderella is not how she did a lot of heavy housework for her wicked sister. The point is a Prince came along and hustled her over to a palace. Where they had electric dishwashers and somebody else to stack them."

The club then rose unanimously and cried: "Hear! Hear!" And, "That's telling 'em!"

When the applause died down, I continued:

"Who did the housework when Cinderella was gone? Who shoveled them ashes? The wicked sisters. The ones who *never* before did any work and just gadded around at parties and such.

"So," I said, "if Labor is such a cool item, the Prince really did them the big favor. He fixed it up so they could do some good, hard, dignified work. And as you can plainly see, dear members of the Redwood Terrace Club, this is nonsense."

There was a pause here for a standing ovation.

Because we have not sold much Kool-Aid and it might spoil anyway, we all had a glass on the house.

The president then took the floor and addressed the speaker and honorary member:

"Daddy, I have to do dishes and fix up my room and all kinds of stuff and I don't think it's fair because I have to go to school and work hard and I think it's mean."

The honorable speaker then put down his glass and said he would address the club further:

"In my previous remarks I may have said things that I would not care to have you ladies carry home to your mothers. For I wish to live in peace on the block.

"As to making beds and cleaning up the dishes, this is hardly work, my dears.

"Consider the wisdom of Marcus Manilius in 40 B.C. who remarked: 'Labor is a pleasure in itself.'

"I call your attention to the immortal Vergil who declared: 'Labor conquers all things.'

"The Democrats in 1880 adopted a platform saying they were friends of Labor. And four years later, the Republican Party denounced imported Labor which might get jobs away from *our* Labor and thereby get too dignified. To say nothing of the pay checks.

"Therefore, dear ladies, you can see that the whole business is rooted in history with some good names around it. So go home and tell your mothers that I told you to be good and do the housework. I thank you."

The club then voted never, never to invite the speaker again and the meeting was adjourned until we call another one.

Mr. W. Parlin Lillard of Chicago meant only for the best, I am sure of that. Nevertheless he put my household in a turmoil.

Mr. Lillard wrote that he had read of the activities of the Redwood Terrace Club which is dedicated to charity through the sale of Kool-Aid. Also to having a real George time like watching TV and catching lizards and keeping them in a glass jar and things like that.

Mr. Lillard wrote that as president of Kool-Aid he was gratified and was sending a package to the membership.

The ladies present thereupon declared they were a committee of the whole. Also a quorum. Also entitled to open the goodie box. Which they did.

The box turned out to contain materials invaluable to the club. Kool-Aid in many delicious flavors; Kool-Shake for making a real George milk shake, kind of; several boxes with things to set up a soft drink stand with caps and aprons and order blanks and things like that, real neat, boy!

The members then laid out these packaged powders all over the living room in order to divide them. And the honorary member and the dog were instructed not to walk on them but to go around the house through the kitchen.

Word was also flashed around the neighborhood and three young ladies came over to join the club. The meeting was interrupted regularly by another young lady who phoned to say why she would *not* join the club. Unless they asked her real nicely.

The members then hooked up the electric blender in the kitchen. And the honorary member and the dog were advised to stay out of the kitchen *and* parlor and to enter the house by shinnying up the roof. Which is real easy.

Also included in the package were little do-it-yourself salad mixes. Several members were detailed to add oil and vinegar and make a lot of dressing.

The honorary member then rose and put his head in the window and spoke as follows:

"Ladies of the club and Madame President: Everything must be cleaned up and put away by bedtime or I will beat the socks off a good many members."

The members then voted to drink Kool-Shakes and watch TV.

The honorary member departed down to the village and is unable to report interim proceedings because the membership had gone to bed by the time he got home again.

The honorary member fetched the car pool this afternoon and was rather alarmed when the president, who happens to be his daughter, was put aboard in wan condition from the school infirmary. He questioned the president as follows:

Q.— "What did you eat?"

A.— "Kool-Shakes."

Q. —"How many?"

A. —"I forget. Five, I think. Maybe six. Then we had Kool-Aid."

Q. —"You drank a lot of Kool-Aid?"

A.— "No, we ate it. Just ate the powder with a spoon. First we had lemon, then grape and then we mixed up raspberry and cherry."

Q.— "How many packages would you say?"

A.— "Most of the box. After I got sick I gave some to the little kids."

Q.— "Heavens-to-Betsy, a box is 48 packages!"

A.— "We ate two boxes."

Q.— "Anything else?"

A.— "We ate two bottles of salad dressing."

Q.— "Did you eat salad, too?"

A.— "No, we didn't have any lettuce, so we ate it with a spoon. We gave some to the cat. She liked it fine."

Q.— "How do you feel now?"

A.— "Hungry."

For something like $9.95, you can buy an iron bowl on wheels and cook in the back yard. Cooking outdoors is considered very elegant these days.

My $9.95 barbecue has an area about the size of a large dishpan.

It chews up $1.90 worth of Mexican charcoal at a clip. And the whole meal, including paint thinner to start the charcoal, costs little more than an evening at a high-class night club.

That is the way we live these days. High on the hog, smoke in the eyes, charcoal over everything.

Outdoor cooking requires a tremendous range of supplementary gear.

The outdoor cook is dressed in chef's hat and a barbecue apron with funny sayings written on it. CRYING TOWEL. WHAT'S YOURS? Things like that. They are expensive. But you cannot do these things with a dish towel wrapped around your waist.

There was a time when we cooked on the stove. But that is all over now, woodsman.

It was a handy thing, the old $500 electrical stove. Those old-timers were not up-to-date. But they had some cute tricks. You just flipped on a switch, put in the meat and let it cook.

Today we load the barbecue with charcoal. The charcoal is then soaked with a special priming fluid ($1.03 a can).

Most of the charcoal I buy could pass fire inspection laws, it is that fire-resistant.

It is a battle all the way between the chef and the asbestos-lined charcoal. A man must be cunning. A pint of gasoline helps a lot.

Some chefs use an electric lighter. This is a sort of hot plate which is placed under the charcoal. It is hot enough to melt lead. And often enough produces a faint glow in the charcoal.

The barbecue is not complete without a spit. Spits are installed by electricians who are trying to pay off their Cadillac in one lump sum.

There is a certain amount of expensive wiring. Since the home builder expected you to live in the home, they put the electricity inside. Silly, wasn't it?

The fuel eventually gets a hot and ruddy complexion. When all the guests begin to cough in the smoke and a faint ash floats down on the martinis, we are ready to cook.

The fodder for these outdoor affairs is usually beef. You can scarcely do anything to hurt beef. But we try hard enough.

The beef is marinated. No self-respecting outdoor cook puts on a steak without giving it several coats of secret lacquer. The steak is beaten with salt and pepper. It is lashed with mustard, glazed and whipped for hours by vestal virgins. At least that is my impression. For the preparation is so secret that a barbecue chef would stab you with a barbecue fork if you asked for the recipe.

The chef is armed with several of these forks. They are so long he needs opera glasses to see whether he is forking the steaks or putting a prong into a guest.

It is a mystic affair. The guests choking and dodging under the smoke. The high priest in his chef's cap, peering through the murk at the offering on the sacred fire.

At a moment determined by stop watches and witchcraft, the chef announces that the food is done.

The guests then tear in hurriedly. If they are smart. For barbecue chills rapidly. A man who could figure the process by which smoking meat reaches deep-freeze temperature by the time you reach the end would make a fortune.

I am surprised the refrigerator people have not looked into this.

This is the way we cook nowadays. In the great, clean, smoky outdoors.

"It makes the food taste so much better," everybody says. "Don't you think so?"

4.

THERE is a mysterious contact between a small boy and the world around him.

I can understand a two-year-old boy trying to put his fingers into the light socket. But how does he know enough to do it while standing barefoot in a puddle of water? We are just one jump from violent electrocution each violent day.

"Don't do that! Do you want to hurt the nice kitty?"

Naturally not. We do not want to hurt the nice kitty. We simply want to throw the nice kitty in the fire. First we put the nice kitty in the red wagon. Then we pull the wagon over by the fire. Then we dump—oops. The nice kitty is agile and jumped out again.

No matter. We will try again. Now, we put the nice kitty in the wagon. And we—

"PUT THAT CAT DOWN!"

Okay. Now let's see. If we filled the tub with water. And

we took the little radio and threw it in the water. Making sure it was hooked up and playing first. . . .

Raising a small girl does not prepare you for a small boy. When my daughter was small, she tried to dress the cat in doll clothes. Many a time I have seen the cat headed down the road with a doll dress flapping and a doll bonnet hanging ridiculously over one ear.

A boy is not interested in dressing a cat. He is interested in hanging the cat. He made a very creditable noose out of some ribbon. I arrived with the reprieve just as the cat was squalling out a free and voluntary confession. Before being hung like a chandelier.

For reasons I cannot figure, the cat *likes* this treatment.

At least he is always hanging around. Practically asking for it. Have you ever seen a determined small boy with a cat's tail and a pair of dull garden scissors?

All that cat did was lie there and watch. Just at the last moment, he would switch his tail. I get gray thinking about it.

My daughter had the soul of an artist. At least if you left any house paint around, she managed to get hold of it and paint the best of the furniture.

A boy—this boy, anyway—a boy is not taken with Art. He is more interested in drinking the paint. Or dunking the cat in it. It is a difference in the sexes, I suppose.

Girls like to dress up. Boys like to dress down. It is very hard to keep pants on a boy. They take them off and stuff them down the yard drain. A yard drain is a challenge to any all-American boy. If you cannot get down it yourself, put your pants down it.

I notice that a small girl does not get at internals the way a boy does.

A girl child will take a playing phonograph. She will seize the delicate arm and rub the needle back and forth across your best records. Scratch!

A boy watches the record go around. Then he gets down underneath and in back. Some manly intuition tells him that you can do twice as much damage. He pries off the back and grabs a handful of wiring. Yank!

He is not content with ruining a record. He wants to wreck the whole machine. (There is another good trick where you drop spoons into the whirling blades of a mixer. We will not go into that.)

Boys are different from girls. You can tell boy children from girl children without looking at the color of their booties.

Leave a girl child in a room with your $50 Swiss travel alarm clock. She will try to eat it. She may drop it. But that is because she is a woman.

A boy child, on the other hand, will *tear it apart* before he eats it.

He does not drop it. He hauls off like an outfielder flinging to home plate. He dashes it against the wall. He is not happy until it begins to drip springs and cog wheels.

Even my daughter at eleven is helpless in the face of such masculinity.

"Come quick! He's eating cigarette butts!"

So he is. I am opposed to children eating cigarette butts. Because you never know when you are going to run out of cigarettes. He is eating the *long* butts, too. Very salvageable items.

The point is, he takes the paper off them first. He likes to look inside.

A girl child would not do that. She would eat them with

the paper on. I know these things from experience and investigation. I am a boy myself.

There are days when I have to control myself to keep from taking clocks apart. It is fascinating what they put inside those things.

You give a small boy a train. He will have it apart and most of the screws lost in an hour. He will have it dismantled while a small girl is still trying to get it in her mouth.

Little girls should not play with toy trains. Neither should little boys, for that matter.

They should sit on the sidelines and *not touch!* While grownups like me show them *how* to play with the train.

For many years I dreamed of a peaceful little home in the country. Nothing gaudy, you understand. A modest home. The sighing of the breeze among the buttercups. The twitter of song birds in the hollyhocks.

By a good deal of frugal living, I achieved this goal.

I did not live frugally but my banker did, thank goodness. By piling up the ready, he was able to lend me what I needed. A pillar of charity, my banker.

I selected a quiet spot. The breeze sighed softly and I auditioned the birds. All on key.

I equipped this nest with every labor-saving device known to man who edits the women's magazines. I shouldn't be bothered with labor while harking to Nature.

What happens? When you turn on these gadgets you CAN HARDLY HEAR YOURSELF THINK!

I have a washing machine. This is very handy. You toss in socks. The machine goes. CHURN, churn, CHURN, churn, CHURN, churn.

It sounds a good deal like a Model-T Ford going up hill. When the washing machine goes off, the labor-saving dryer goes on. The dryer has a steady mmmmmmmmmmmmmmmmmmmmmmmmmm. For some reason, it is in sympathetic tune with a chandelier. The chandelier has a metal shade that rattles in tune with the dryer. Click, click, click, click, click.

An electric fan draws the heat and smoke off the stove. Wheeeeeeeeeeeeee.

The labor-saving dishwasher has a peculiar timing. Sssssssss. In goes the water. Brp, brp, brp, brp, brp. The internals perform some mysterious function. There is a gulping sound as the water drains out.

Then silence. A red electric eye on this infernal machine continues to glow. The machine is not sleeping. It is gathering strength for the next cycle. *Whoosh!* Sssssssssss. Glurp! Brp, brp, brp, brp, brp.

I have a vacuum cleaner that sets the teeth on edge. It sounds like a saw running up against a nail. I could hardly live without it, though. It is so labor-saving.

My furnace is automatic. When the heat goes down to a certain point, the automatic pilot switches on the heat. *Plop!* Immediately things inside the closet begin to crackle.

I am assured that this is just expansion of casing and so forth. But I am extremely nervous about such things. Something is going to blow and I know it.

There are times when all these devices fall silent. Everything is washed and dried. Everything is clean. The chandelier stops quivering. The red electric eyes blink off.

You can open the windows. And by golly, you can hear the birds. Yes, you can. Tweet, tweet, tweet. It is mightly pastoral and lovely.

In that lovely silence, there is only the faint whine of the refrigerator.

At this point things begin to crackle. Why? Because now they are contracting! That is what the man said. They crackle when they get hot because they are expanding. They crackle when they get cold because they contract.

My picture of this house is something like a whale breathing.

Pooft! Hissssssssssss.

"Good heavens, what's that?"

"Just the hot water heater going on."

The water heats and the fire goes out with another *pooft.*

I should report that this makes my banker very happy. I am a solid citizen with plenty of labor saved. The fact that I am hollow-eyed and leap three feet in the air at a touch has nothing to do with it.

I am a modern man. All modern men leap three feet into the air at times. They have plenty of energy left over from all the labor they have saved up.

Click, click, click, click. Pooft. Plop. Whosh. Wheeeee!

We were all up at daybreak to go and watch the movie *The Darkest Hour* being made on San Francisco Bay. I had promised the youthful fan of my household that we would see Mr. Alan Ladd foil Mr. Edward G. Robinson.

We were up at daybreak because it takes a good deal of time to dress for such an important occasion. The business of going to pieces over dress starts early.

"Will Mr. Ladd speak to me?"

"If he doesn't I will never speak to him," I said loyally.

"I'm so nervous," she said. "Oh, I'm so nervous. And my gloves aren't clean. Is my hat on straight? What shall I say?"

"Anything," I said. "So long as it is polite. Your hat looks elegant. Straw sailors are very becoming to you. Hold your gloves in your hand. If you can't think of anything to say, smile."

"I can't," she said desperately. "He'd see the bands on my teeth."

The company of *The Darkest Hour* was working at a float near Fisherman's Wharf. It was the clincher scene. A police boat comes roaring in. Mr. Alan Ladd gets out looking very stern. Two cops hustle out Mr. Edward G. Robinson. He looks mad.

A pretty lady comes down the gangplank onto the float. Mr. Ladd puts his arms around her. They walk off together.

"Who's that? The lady."

"That's Miss Joanne Dru."

"*Joanne Dru?* Oh, my goodness!"

"Kindly hold down your voice," I said nervously. "At your age it has a tendency to sound like a steam whistle."

"But Joanne Dru! Oh, my gosh!"

A press agent came over and asked if we would like to meet Miss Dru. I held onto the fan before she could fall on the deck.

Miss Dru was sitting in a big limousine waiting while the electricians did long, involved things with lights and reflectors. She said she had an eleven-year-old daughter herself. She wondered if this one had lost all her teeth yet.

This one came out of some dream world and snapped her mouth shut over the bands.

The boat came roaring in again. The cameras turned.

Mr. Ladd got out looking stern. Mr. Robinson got out look-ing mad. Miss Dru got out of the limousine and ran down the gangplank.

"Let's do it again," said the director. "You don't look wet enough."

Mr. Ladd and Mr. Robinson came up while a man with a hose sprayed them with water. The press agent explained that Mr. Ladd is a cop, wrongly sent to prison. He gets out and has a terrible fight with Mr. Robinson who is the head of some bad fishermen. They fall in the bay.

"I stood there. Right beside her," said the fan in an awed voice. "She had curlers in her hair."

Mr. Ladd sat down on a stringer and was introduced, drip-ping. He said he had an eleven-year-old daughter, too.

"How old are you?"

"Ten, no, twelve. Oh, gosh, I mean eleven."

Mr. Ladd got up and went back to sea again. The boat roared up. He got out looking stern. Mr. Robinson got out looking mad. Miss Dru ran down the plank. They kissed.

"Mushy," murmured the fan. She murmured it with ap-proval, though.

It could happen to any girl. We hope. She stood there knock-kneed with one hand in a soiled white glove hold-ing down the sailor hat. She was smiling. A little bandy about the teeth, but plenty of soul in it.

You cannot keep up with what the ladies are doing unless you read the ladies' magazines. There are some great thoughts between the cake mix and the floating girdle ads, believe me.

"Household finances usually do better if handled by the distaff side," says the author authority. "Women seem to have a knack for these things."

Well, aside from hollow laughter—and if I went around writing things like "distaff side," my family would be in the poorhouse within a month—aside from that, I would like to know more about this knack.

Most ladies I know have a knack for getting furious with the bank when the monthly statement does not agree with their own peculiar bookkeeping. I guess that is a knack.

In fact, I am sure that it is a knack. It is not mathematics. I do not know what else you could call it.

"First, I deposited a $50 check," says Madam chewing her pencil. "Then I paid the grocer $14.25 and the shoes cost $31.99 on sale and—"

"What is this $7.50 scratchout?" says the breadwinner.

"That was $7.50 that I put in only I spent it. So it cancels itself out."

Now, if you have the knack, it seems when you deposit something and then it cancels itself, you can go on spending it over and over. Because it cancels itself out—can't you see that?

"You can only spend it *once*," says the working man. "Heavens-to-Betsy, if you keep on spending it and canceling it, no wonder it doesn't come out."

The lady with the knack begins to quiver. With rage, with emotion, maybe with knack. Who knows?

"You don't love me!"

It is very social these days to let the lady handle the finances. And we are social as all get out. Even if it kills us and the banker too.

97

I have just looked it up in Amy Vanderbilt whose book solves all my social problems:

> A husband, talented as he may be in his own field, may also have difficulty in the handling of money and, if so, should be helped toward the organizing of his obligations.
> A general vagueness on the part of, say, a creative artist concerning the mundane matters of existence makes him in no way inferior to his mate who may be able to read a balance sheet at a glance.

Thank you. Thank you.

The main difficulty your creative artist finds about money is that it is so vague. In fact, there is not enough of it. That is my difficulty.

Now as to reading a balance sheet at a glance. I point silently to the settling of the luncheon check. Mesdames have discussed the current trends of Balmain. They have cut up all ladies not present and wondered "how in the world she puts on such airs with her husband's salary."

Now the check, please.

"Let me see. Who had the chicken salad? That's 90 cents and the sales tax is 3½ cents. Well, just give me the 93 cents and never mind the half.

"You had soup and the fish. Oh, did you see last month's copy of *Glut*? This fish dish sounds divine. You cook it in a court bouillon or maybe it was parsley. Now dessert was extra on yours because you didn't order the regular lunch.

"So that comes to—has anybody got a pencil?—it comes to $5.23. Now why does the check say $6.85? There must be some mistake. Here, you give me a dollar and I'll give you back 12 cents and that makes that even."

This is financial wizardry. And it takes more than a knack, honey. What it takes is cash.

There is something between a small boy and a cow. And on the first sunny days of summer we go in search of cows.

The cows hang over the fence and look at the small boy.

The small boy hangs out the car window and looks at the cows—we stop the car and I keep a grip on the seat of his pants.

Across the strip of green grass and the barbwire fence, love is established.

"Hi, cow!"

The cow does not reply. But you can see by the look in her eye she is thinking loving thoughts.

If you have a very small boy, the search for cows can go on all day. Each new cow is as delightful as the very first one.

If there are whole herds of cows, we take them one by one. It takes time but is worth every loving glance. Horses come next. After that, sheep. Then ducks.

I would like to find a place where they milk cows. All small boys should have that experience. The cow standing peacefully in the dark barn. And the man with his head against the cow's side and the milk going into the pail with that wonderful hissing sound.

I think cows hand over their milk to machines these days. But when I was a small boy in love with cows, they milked by hand. While the cow was being milked, all the farm cats stood around meowing.

Once in a while, the milker would turn the stream of milk toward the cats. The cats would stand on their hind legs and catch the warm milk in their mouths. Seeing that is an experience that stays with you all your life.

The cows in the pasture these days are mainly brown and white. Just like the nursery rhyme of the cow: "I love with all my heart . . . she gives me cream with all her might . . . to eat with apple tart."

I am teaching this to my son. And one of these days will find a place where they milk cows. And give some to the cats. And so this great emotion will not be lost.

After the milking, the pails were emptied in a sort of washtub (when I was fond of cows). The cream gathered on top and was skimmed off. Grandpa said you could lift it off "like a pair of britches."

While this child is absorbing cows, I would not want him to grow up without seeing cream come off the top "like a pair of britches."

Cows have become subject to automation, like everything else. But I imagine somewhere there is a cow and a milker. And tortoise-shell cats and a dark barn with a hayloft.

I find in my cow file that one of the champion cows of our nation was named Bessie. She lived at Princeton, N. J. One year, she manufactured—that is the word they use around cows currently—manufactured 14,496 quarts of milk. Also 1,930 pounds of butter.

This is a splendid record. But it is a terrible waste of milk if all they did was put it in waxed cartons and deliver it to front doors.

With 14,496 quarts of milk, you could entertain heaven knows how many small boys. To say nothing of cats.

Anyway, that is the way we spend our summer days. In rich and satisfying emotion between boy and cow.

I have lost the touch, myself. I look at the cow and the cow looks at me. Something has been there. But it is gone.

But when the boy looks at the cow and the cow looks at the boy, I remember. Oh, yes, I remember that.

Since you can't take it with you, a good many people make wills. I have made a will and I must say it is a heart-warming thing. My daughter is entranced with my will. She can hardly wait for me to pop off so she can see what is in the grab bag.

For many years, I read English novels how all the crusty aunts and the evil nephews sat around and were very nice to the old Earl. The old Earl sat around and was constantly having in his solicitors.

A solicitor is a kind of a lawyer. A cut below a barrister, I gather. When the solicitor would show up at old Shoulder Arms, the family would know somebody else was being named to get the estate and the pearls.

It was very good reading.

"Change your will today, m'Lordship?"

"Why, yes, Wamley, b'lieve I will, by jove. Jolly good idea, what?"

Well, with a little imagination and practically no capital, you can do the same thing.

My daughter thinks of me as being quite wealthy. And I have done nothing to discourage this. Who am I to fling cold water on her small dreams? At one time I sought obedience with the back of a hairbrush. These days I simply threaten to change my will.

"I have left you all my shirts. You know the ones you wear

with the tails outside? But if you are not a good girl, I will leave them to the laundryman."

"When will I get them?"

"When your poor old father goes to his reward," I say solemnly. "Which may be any day now since I am feeling right poorly. The thing for you to do is hang on and coddle me. Make me so happy I don't have to call in my solicitor and change my will for amusement."

I believe in keeping the bait fresh and not too far out of reach.

The other day I found something amazing in the newspaper.

"One half of all professional people fail to make a will with pharmacists leading the list and journalists second."

This is interesting information. Either it shows that I am not a true journalist or I am a man of unusual foresight.

I do not know why pharmacists do not make wills. I suspect it is because they have so much free aspirin, they do not think they might knock off. When I get a cold, for instance, I know I am going to die. And I would too, except for the greatest will power ever seen by medical science.

For a pharmacist, a cold is just a good reason to get one of the fringe benefits of the job. Free aspirin. He dips into the aspirin barrel and gets himself a couple of little old tablets and gulp.

Never cost him a cent.

A journalist being delicately constructed and without free aspirin should make a will. Especially if he has small children in the house.

There was a hero of our times who declared: "If I can't take it with me, I won't go."

But I am not made of such stern stuff. And on gloomy Mondays when the typewriter seems to have all the wrong keys and the poison oak is itching again, I find great comfort in the things I shall leave behind.

"My white shirts. And my watch and my screw driver so you can take it apart. *All* my money in the bank which, at the rate of your modest 50 cents a week allowance, will keep you in Hershey bars for some years.

"There are my cuff links and my boots which you can grow into. My tuxedo which would be terribly handy for Halloween parties. Oh, there are all kinds of goodies in my will. But you must be very good to me," I say, "or I will have in my solicitor and maybe leave my bow ties to the dog."

By this means, we have laid up a good deal of interest in my failing health and the possibility of getting hit by a truck.

Sometimes we can hardly wait.

Well, when President Kennedy hears this, he will have cat fits. But if I have told the Government once, I have told them a hundred times: I cannot add and I cannot subtract.

It seems I have overpaid my income tax. *Overpaid!*

"You have paid taxes on $1,000 you never got," said the Money Man.

"How could I do that, Money Man?"

"It is one of life's mysteries," said the Money Man with a sigh. "It seems you added two and two and got five."

Let me tell you this is the advantage of having a Money Man. A Money Man is a new thing in our lives. A Money Man looks at your money. And he tells you why it is not more than you hoped it would be.

"Let us sue the Government at once, Money Man," I said. "When I am on the shorts, the Federal bagmen are very curt with me. They talk of attachments and even hint they would put me in the Federal slammer.

"Relations with my Government should be a two-way street," I said. "How much can we get back?"

The Money Man said we could reopen the deal and possibly put in for a couple of bills.

"Or maybe even $250," he said. "But I would not advise it."

"That is no way to talk about my money, Money Man. Why not?"

"As soon as you amend your tax return," he said, "the Government will examine you. Have you ever been examined?"

"Yes, sir."

"What did the Government say?"

"They said: 'L-A, soldier.'"

The Money Man said this was not what he meant. "When you are examined for income tax, it is a terrible experience. You must come up with memory you have forgotten and receipts that do not exist.

"Once the Federals have got your first money, they are unhappy about letting go of it. They will give it back if you insist. But they will rack you up considerably in the process."

As if this were not enough to curdle the milk on your Wheaties, what should happen today but the Government sends a check for $27.35!

There is no explanation for this check. It simply says: TAX RETURN.

The check is green. It is made of some kind of cardboard.

It is punched with a lot of slits that go through the IBM machine—these slits tell the Government *everything* but tell me *nothing*.

I point out to my Government that $27.35 is not two bills. Not what I have coming when I overpaid.

That is, I would tell my Government that. If I dast. But I do not dast.

"This makes it even worse," groaned the Money Man.

"Let us burn the check secretly at midnight, Money Man."

"Don't touch it," he said. "Hold everything while I think."

Well, this is what happens when the Government lets me add and subtract.

If I ask for my money back, the bagmen will turn me inside out.

If I cash this little old check, I may be committing all kinds of IBM slit crime. I do not know where I am. And the Government is not telling me.

"It is very bad to underpay your tax," said the Money Man. "But it is even worse to overpay. We will just have to sit tight and see if the Government comes through with an explanation."

"But what about my money, Money Man? That was my problem when I came in."

"That is what I have been telling you," he said. "The Government has your money. And, you will be lucky if they just keep it."

The decorator comes tomorrow. And I hardly know what to tell him.

My home is in a constant state of decoration. Chairs are at

a premium. For mostly my chairs are out being re-covered. Furniture is as constantly on the move as a wheat-harvest bum. Pictures hang, disappear, reappear in other rooms. Throw rugs are replaced by wall-to-wall carpeting.

Just about the time I am sure-footed again, the throw rugs are back. And we are skidding from one to the other, like Liza crossing the ice.

It keeps a man agile and active. I will say that.

Now what do I read in magazines but decorating is very difficult on ladies. It upsets their mental equilibrium and gets them all jittery inside.

"Decorating a home puts a woman under tremendous psychic pressure," says the doctor-writer in the magazine. "And in doing so, brings to the surface her underlying weaknesses."

He then goes on to prove his point. And if you could read what he says about ladies who have a lot of clocks in the house, you would be surprised. Surprised and interested.

All sorts of things go on when a lady decorates a house. It is not just a question of shoving the couch into the center of the room and putting in a couple of end tables with lamps.

The lady is not really decorating. She is solving her inside problems.

The medic tells of a lady with bowlegs. Naturally she felt badly about this, bowlegs being out of style for ladies. (Though very good for cowboys. My boy tries to make his legs bow.)

The lady started out by decorating the front room with bowlegged chairs. The brocaded kind named after one of the French Louis Kings. The ones you sit down on and everybody screams: *"Don't tilt it!"*

Well, the lady was uncomfortable. (Though why I don't know, since they matched her own legs.) So then she got straight spindly-legged chairs. (The kind you sit in and the hostess grinds her teeth and says: "Don't you think you'd be more comfortable on the couch?")

This did not work either. And the bowlegged lady felt all out of kilter.

Finally she got big blocky chairs with no legs at all! Then she felt simply grand.

Personally, this sounds like a terrible way to live. And if ladies must struggle with the furniture in direct ratio to their soul struggles, it is obvious we are going to have a pretty untidy living room.

When the lady is exhausted from the psychic hammerlock, she calls in the doctor—the decorator.

This, says the doctor-writer, is a big mistake.

The decorator has his own problems. Instead of one catch-as-catch-can psyche in the home, you now have two.

Pretty soon everybody is screaming at each other.

Who takes the final fall? The ever-loving breadwinner who spends his Sundays pushing the furniture back and forth. Trying to find a spot where it fits Madam's tender trauma.

Nevertheless, the decorating man cometh. Come the bright tomorrow morning. And I do not know whether to let the serpent in. Or shotgun him off the property.

It is hard to argue this proposition. Since all the ladies I know in my neighborhood are up to the Plimsoll mark in swatches and wallpaper and decorators. It is an accepted form of life. And if you suggested to all these delicate primroses they should quit moving furniture and mend their ways, you are a boor.

And though this visit is advertised as a mere installation of a coffee table, I know better. It will wind up with the TV moved so you have to crack your neck to look at it. The reading light will be gone from my reading chair. And replaced by an ottoman. ("Don't put the ash tray on it. You might burn it!")

It will be about as comfortable as a boxcar. But our souls will be at peace.

I bought a vine—I think it is a Virginia creeper, though frankly I don't care at this point. I bought it on sale for $1.39 at the nursery. All my neighbors envied me my good luck. Theirs died while my $1.39 flourished to about $10.50 worth.

It climbed the house like a second-story burglar.

That was the problem. At the second story it stopped to catch its breath. And since then it has been climbing down again.

I am informed that this vine needs continual boosting. Like getting a small boy over a fence.

"The vine has to be nailed up," said the nurseryman. "Keep nailing it up as it climbs."

Now it so happens that I did not equip the outside of my house with Jacob's ladders. Not figuring I was building an ark but rather a residence for declining years.

"How would you go about nailing it up?" I asked politely.

"Get a long ladder," said the nurseryman.

I went down and priced long ladders. Long ladders cost more per foot than acreage on Broadway.

"Would you like to buy back the vine?" I asked desperately.

"All sales are final," said the nurseryman. "By the way, use big nails."

This vine at present is grasping in all directions. But mostly downhill. It gives no impression of a vine-covered cottage. But rather looks as though a whole clump of old greenery had been thrown out the window and hung up on a nail.

One straying runner of it got into the storm gutters where a bird nested in it. The gutter is now clogged and can only be cured with a long ladder.

I could have joined the fire department and led the same kind of life. Got paid for it, too.

I should mention trees. I have put in several trees. Though I am fearful of what will happen when they grow up.

I had trees already. Madrones, live oaks, bay and redwood. These trees overhung the homesite and gave it a shady suburban air.

No sooner was the house built than these trees began to get little ailments. They shivered and cast off limbs and required constant attention of tree doctors. The closer ones faded entirely and now threaten to cast a ton or more of dead limbs through the roof.

"What can I do?" I asked on the telephone.

"Well," said the tree man, "you get a long ladder . . ."

It is obvious that a man with a house should buy climbing irons and take trapeze lessons.

There is nothing that happens to this house that is within reach. I spend hours hanging out the window trying to lasso vines, birds' nests, stray limbs and other natural bric-a-brac. It is a precarious life.

This is the way an innocent housing project worked out

for me. A future on a long, long ladder, nailing up a long, long vine.

Creep back to Virginia, you creeper.

Life is hard on the younger generation. This is the day we trudge wearily back to school in my household.

Trudging wearily is just a poetic way of putting it. Actually the trudging is done in a high-powered car pool. And the weariness is supplied mainly by me who cannot get accustomed to early hours.

I shall not have to do it after this first day. At least not for a while. The thirteen-year-old scholar hereabouts will be a boarder for the first month. This is supposed to keep her mind on her work. I am hopeful but far from confident.

Some people have minds that can be hung on a problem and stay there.

Then there are the other kind. The kind I am packing off to the halls of learning. With best wishes.

I don't know how any thirteen-year-old keeps her mind on anything more than five minutes these days. There are so many distractions. So many things to keep your mind on. It wears you out.

There is the whole field of romance, for instance.

At thirteen, a child has double work. Leaping from comic books to *True Life Romances*. From "Artie and His Pen Pals" to "I Married a Sleepwalker." A child is too exhausted to dip into schoolbooks after a hard day like this.

"There were these twins, you know? And Stella was in love with this boy. Only Pam, her twin, was in love with him too. Because they were exact twins. And they *had* to feel the same way, you know?"

"So what happened?"

"Well, Pam thought she should give him up. Because Stella gave her her kidney."

"Her what?"

"Pam had this disease or something, I think. Anyway, Stella—I mean Pam had this operation and the only way she could live was with her twin's kidney. So she gave it to her."

"Wrapped for Christmas?"

"Oh, Father! Anyway this boy went out with Pam. Only he really thought he was going out with Stella, you know? So Pam didn't tell him. Because she was *so* in love with him. What would you have done?"

"I would have said, 'Madam, which twin has the kidney?' Is this really in that magazine? Or are you making it up?"

"It is true," she said. "It's in *True Romances*. Everything in it is true."

"I don't think you should read such magazines. Tell me, what happened then?"

"Oh, it's so *sad*. Stella was killed in this auto accident, you know? Now the boy thinks Pam is Stella. Only Pam doesn't know what to do. She is hiding in seclusion."

"You mean it ends there?" I cried. "How will I sleep to-night? Not knowing how it all ended happily ever after."

"She is in seclusion," said the child firmly. "And she wants everybody to write to her what she should do."

Well, that is what is taking up most of our time these days. We can hardly keep our mind on fractions. When a lady with a borrowed kidney is in seclusion waiting for our letter.

There are simply not enough hours in the day. Not enough to solve heartbreak and the square inches enclosed by a par-allelogram both. In an emergency like this, the area figure must go over the tailgate. And we are upstairs, writing like mad with the old ball-point.

DEAR PAM: I have read your problem. It is a terrible problem. I think you should . . .

This is the Year of the Dog. It is Year 4656 in the Chinese calendar.

How this word got around to my dog I will never know. My dog cannot claim a touch of Chow or Lhasa terrier, not that pure, scupper-lipped boxer, name of Mike.

Nevertheless, he has decided that this is his year.

It is also Small Boy year. They will split the year between them.

We have a new game at my house. The Small Boy gets in a closet and shuts the door. I sneak over tippy-toed. I *jerk* open the door! The Small Boy collapses in shrieks of laughter.

It is a simple game. Not much brains are required.

This game goes on and on. And on and on and on and on. This child finds something he likes, he sees no point in changing it.

"Wouldn't you like to play with the nice choo-choo?"

No sir. He just goes and hides in the closet again. Open the door! Ha, ha, ha, ha, ha!

I get very tired of this game. But I have little staying power. After about two dozen times of opening the closet door, I have had it. It loses its charm.

For the Small Boy it is just getting good. It has a lot of build-up. The screams of delight increase. The more you do it, the better it gets.

I should report that all this was quietly driving the dog daffy.

This dog has very little sense. But he latches onto things. He is a very responsible dog about things he latches onto. When he latched onto the new Siamese kittens, it got so their own mother had to have a permit to see them. He was worse than a maternity ward nurse.

At present, the dog is latched onto the Small Boy. Apparently all this screaming affected the dog's nerves. For all he knew, I was sticking pins in the child.

He stood around muttering and getting in the way.

Finally he bit me. He bit me in an apologetic way. Then he tried to pass it off as a joke—you know, jumping on me and acting like a puppy.

Well, I was about to haul off and knock that dog bowlegged. But I looked at his teeth and decided to hold a conference at the summit.

"Mike! You should be ashamed!"

The dog hung his head. But he was not fooled. He knew he had me bluffed. I could see him watching me.

I can take this bum, he was thinking. One more jump at the kid and he's hamburger.

Every time I reached for the door handle, the child yelled. Every time the child yelled, the dog growled. It was very embarrassing. When you cannot harry your own child and your own dog drives you off—well.

After a while the child came out of the closet.

He could not figure why I did not wish to play such a fascinating game.

That two-faced dog was all for shaking hands and making up. Such cavorting around and trying to pretend it never happened. I would not be caught dead shaking hands with such a dog. Not even in the Year of the Dog.

He went over and looked the child over very carefully. To see I had not broken off any arms or legs. He gave him a good lick on the face.

The child was not grateful. He hauled off and gave the dog a good kick in the ribs. The dog loved it.

I wish I had the nerve to kick that dog in the ribs. I would give him a belt he would not forget. But I do not have the nerve. I know it. And he knows it. In this Year of the Dog.

5.

DEAR DAIRY:

Our Father bought us a dairy. He said if we wrote in it every day it would be very valuable in later years.

If anybody reads what we wrote in our dairy, they will have very back luck and catch something terrible. Today we went to school. We got an A minus in history. There is a girl in our class who can wiggle her ears. It is horrible but kind of neat.

We asked our Father where to hide our dairy. He said when he was a boy he hid it under the mattress. He said that was the best place.

We hid our dairy in another place. It is so secret that we will not even write it down. If we were captured, like in war —you know like in the movies—we would not tell.

We are nearly grown up. This year we are going to get a job. We think maybe in the movies or maybe being a waitress.

We asked our Father where to get a job.

He said: "What for? Is it possible you intend to support your poor old parent in his declining years?"

We said we needed money for Christmas presents.

"How much do you require for your Yuletide?" he inquired from us.

We said we needed $50 dollars. We said we would take a job from him. We would sharpen pencils and do real neat things like that.

He said $50 dollars? "May I politely inquire if you are going into partnership with Harry Winston on the Hope diamond?" he inquired politely.

He is real weird sometimes. I mean honestly!

The reason we need $50 dollars, dear dairy, is we need to buy a horse.

We asked our Father how long it would take to save up and buy a horse.

He said he has already bought a whole herd of horses in cans to feed our dog. He said the dog has not done a lick of real work in his whole life and he does not intend to spend his existence buying thousands of horses for us to ride and the dog to eat.

He said he is a poor man and barely able to keep body and soul together.

When he talks like that we do not bother him anymore. We wait until after dinner. After dinner sometimes when we have wine he gets very excited.

He will buy you anything. Once he had martinis before dinner and wine, too. He promised to buy us a car!

Next day though he said we had taken advantage of him in his misery. Anyway, he said, he meant he would buy us a car when we were 21. If we did the dishes without complaining and got better marks, he meant. Gee! He is not fair. I mean really. We will *never* get to be 21!

DEAR DAIRY:

We went to school. It was real gishy. Horrible! We wish we were 15 years old. It is a keen age. Fourteen is no good because nobody will take you seriously or give you a job or anything.

Our Father is not a poor man like he says. We think he has $50 dollars. We asked him if you could buy a horse for $50 dollars. He said to go figure how much a can of dog food cost and then multiply.

He said: "It is simply a matter of determining how many cans of dog food there is in a horse and I am surprised they do not teach you these practical matters in your school," he said excitedly.

We will ask him again after dinner.

We did our homework. Ugh! They do not tell you how much horses cost. Our Father said if we could get a job on TV with a horse, he would ask the bank to lend him some money and buy the horse. That would be eepy! Only he is so weird sometimes you cannot believe what he says. Just sometimes real nice and other times real glunky. Gosh!

DEAR DAIRY:

This year we are all 14 and going to high school. During the summer we were supposed to write a book review. Only we forgot until yesterday.

We told our Father please buy a book called *Mama's Bank Account.* We told him he could buy it in a paper back because we are trying to save him money. He got real mad and said how the Sam Hill would he find a paper back of the book? And he doubted if there was a paper back of this book because all the paper backs he sees look like they are about the chorus line at the Mocambo or anyway a warm climate.

He is weird. I mean, really!

This summer at the lake we got up on water skis. It was real neat!

The records we would like most to have are "Teddy Bear" by Elvis Presley and "Send for Me" by Nat "King" Cole and "Shake, Baby, Shake," by Elvis Presley and "Rebel" by Carol Jarvis.

The other night we put on a party dress and our Father had to button it up the back. He said he little thought he has been nursing a viper in his bosom. And he said he has spent more time buttoning people up the back than he has put into his business and that is why he is poor and not rich.

He is weird sometimes. I really mean it.

This summer in a magazine it said something about a girl, you know? And she lost her arms. And so she learned to paint pictures with her feet and became a famous artist!

Sometimes we sort of wish we had no arms and could paint pictures with our feet. We don't really—but it would be neat to be a famous artist.

Our Father said he knew a 14-year-old girl once. He said:

"She used her Father's electric razor to shave her legs. She did it while she was talking on the telephone for hours to her friends. When she looked down she had shaved off both her legs."

He said she became a famous artist and had to paint with her arms.

He felt real pleased with himself and went around laughing. If he is in a good humor all day, we will ask him to buy the records for us.

We got *Mama's Bank Account* and read it. In the review where you put down "Underlying Theme" we wrote:

"This moving and enchanting story is altogether irresistible because they thought they had a bank account but they didn't."

Our Father said: "Where did you get all that moving and enchanting and irresistible stuff?" We said we made it up. Then he demanded to look at the book and inside the cover it said something like that. Only we said "moving and enchanting" and they said "enchanting and moving."

Our Father grabbed at his forehead and said if this ever got out he would be ruined. He said:

"At my age I should raise a daughter as a plagiarist!"

He was real weird. I'm not kidding. Really!

We washed our hair and our Father got real mad because we used the whole tube of his shampoo. But we had to tear the tube anyway to get the soap out so it would not have been any good to him at all. Gee.

Our hair looks terrible! Nothing helps. While we were washing, we could hear our Father saying:

"One hour! I give you my word I timed it and she has been looking in the mirror a solid hour!"

Our Father made a new rule when we talk on the telephone. We must take the egg timer and we can only turn it over once then we must get off the phone. The stuff in the egg timer looks like salt.

We asked our Father if we could take it apart. He said,

why? We told him because we would like to put some pepper in it. So it would be like half salt and half pepper. It would be real neat!

Our Father said something we cannot repeat. And he said he thought he would go out and find a quiet saloon and meditate. We asked him if he would pick up a record "Over the Mountain" by Elvis Presley. It's the neatest!

DEAR DAIRY:

I am getting tired of picking up all the time. They are always yelling at me: "Pick this up." And, "Pick that up." Then *they* drop things all over the house themselves. I wish we had a maid. Like in the movies. Gee!

Our Father said: "A maid is a great sign of social success and I wish we had one too," he remarked thoughtfully. He said if he could get one on time payments he would be tempted. But our banker will hardly loan him the price of a cup of coffee.

He said he is into our banker for the next 50 years. And the only comforting thought is that he does not expect to live that long at this pace.

"We will see then who laughs last," he laughed.

Our Father said to write down everything that happens in our dairy. It would be a record of our times. Nothing much happened. We went to school. Penelope has a new hair-do. It looks weird. They do not have a maid either.

We saw a real cool picture at the show. This lady was in love, you know? Only it was with the wrong man but she learned her lesson in time. She had a maid. The maid put bath salts in her tub. Boy!

Our Father said he was used to maids. He said when he

was a boy they had so many servants around the house he was always falling over them.

He said: "I was raised in the lap of luxury and spent all my time on the estate out in Long Island. Except when we took the yacht and went down to Florida."

He said he never had to worry what to wear because their social secretary figured out what they should do each day. Like going fox hunting or playing polo.

I do not think it is true. Grandmother says he has a vivid imagination. She said the only help they had was a hired girl who came in when they had company.

She said our Father did not pick up around the house, either. He was sloppy.

Once we had a big party and a caterer man came to help us. He wore a white coat and passed around champagne and little things to eat.

Our Father went out in the kitchen and began talking to him. We could hear them laughing and laughing. They were drinking some of the champagne and eating the things.

Everybody was very fussy at our Father afterwards.

He said for heaven's sake it turned out the caterer man had been a waiter on the same ship he was on. Only at different times.

He said: "What is the spirit of friendship coming to when a man cannot hold a friendly chat with an old shipmate in his own house?" he said quietly.

Next night he brought home a box of candy and was very polite.

Our Father says if we get a maid will we please get one who also rubs backs. He says his back is giving him fits. I asked him why. He said probably because everybody is on it and sometimes he feels like Atlas. Only weaker.

We said we would rub his back.

He said: "Thank you, no, it is too tender," he said tenderly.

He said would I kindly pick up the papers. Gosh! *He* was the one who put them there.

He said it did not matter. He said: "I am a doddering old man whose back has been sacrificed to upholding our social position. And picking up the papers is a small return for the best years of my life." Weird!

He said he would buy some bath salts. And he put on a bath towel on his head and went prancing around. Acting like he was a maid. It was so funny! And I do not see how he can run around like that if his back hurts like he says. Gosh!

Dear Dairy:

Our Father is on vacation. He said: "Vacation is just like any other time. Only everybody thinks all you have to do is drive people around like a blooming chauffeur and write, too."

We forgot to buy hair spray. He drove us down to the drugstore to get some. He is very grumpy. We hope vacation will end soon.

Our Father said: "If you ever marry a column writer, be sure you get one who has a dodge where there are plenty of guest columnists. Otherwise, he will be worn out ere the bloom is off his youth."

We do not intend to marry a column writer. We will marry a farmer. One who has horses we can ride.

Our Father said he wishes he had a column on books. He said: "It is one of the best ways to get guest columnists. Because everybody has an idea he is a book critic. Also they will work for nothing plus a free book."

We said it is easy to write a column. Because there are lots of things to write about.

He looked at us in a queer way and said: "What have I done to deserve this viper in my bosom?"

He is wild! I mean, gol-ly! We hope his vacation will end soon.

For our vacation we went down in the Cachagua valley. We rode a horse named Sugar. He is a keen horse.

We went to a party the other night. Our Father had to drive us. He moaned and groaned and said he intended to resign and become a taxi driver. Only with a meter on the car and get paid for it.

Nobody can speak to him when he is on vacation.

He sits at the typewriter and tears paper out of it and throws it in the basket and makes the funniest noises.

He says he wishes he was a saloon columnist. He would sit all day in a cool saloon and on vacation he would pick important people out of the saloon and they would write guest columns.

He said that is the way they do it at Toots Shor's in New York. And he said he knows half a dozen writers he bets cannot write their own names any more because they are so loaded with guest columnists.

We think it is disgusting. I mean, honestly!

Our Father said it is a good idea to write "we" when you are writing like this. He said: "It sounds like you have two heads."

We are 15 at last! Some people treat us like an individual. Not like a child. Not our Father, though. We tried to tell him politely. He said, heartily: "Mind your manners. You are spilling the soup." Gosh!

Our allowance is still not enough. Even with money we make baby-sitting.

We spoke to our Father about it. He gave us a long lecture on the value of money. He said he would be fried in oil if he interfered with our allowance because it was all worked out on higher levels.

Then he lent us a dollar and said, heavenly days, don't tell anyone about it. He is all right sometimes. Only very strange. We will buy some keen new hair spray with the money.

Our Father said if we kept spraying our hair, our head will get so stiff it will break off. And he said he is afraid to lay a hand on us for fear we are brittle.

We said would he mind driving us to the swimming pool. He yelled like he was crazy or something and tore his paper out of the typewriter.

Gosh! He is on vacation. We hope it will end soon. It is unbearable. I mean, really!

6.

OUR Siamese cat has been located. After many an anguished day and many an anxious night.

This cat's name is Freddy—that is what the children insisted on calling him. I thought it was a poor name for a cat. Sounded like somebody who wore spats and went around saying, "Pip, pip."

The kids thought it was a fine name, however. Maybe it suited him at that. He was a beautiful cat. But one of the most lame-brained animals I ever saw.

Freddy disappeared about three weeks ago. Just wandered up the hillside under the oaks as usual—what he did I never knew. He was too proud to work. Quail used to walk right in front of him.

All it did was remind him to come in and get me to open a can of Dr. Ross.

He wandered off up the hill. And he didn't come back.

Heavens-to-Betsy, the dramatics that went on!

"He's probably dead!"

"He is not," I said. "He is probably out mousing around some lady cat. If he has that much sense, which I doubt. That cat will come back."

"How can you talk like that? When poor Freddy may be killed!"

There is nothing girl children like better than thinking of the horrors of life.

Poor Freddy was pictured in snow and rain. (It never rains here in the summer and there hasn't been snow in a hundred years. But no matter.)

We pictured poor Freddy at grips with a mountain lion.

We pictured him lost and without two sticks to rub together. Mewing piteously.

Well, it turns out Freddy simply went up the hill and took up with rich neighbors. And when he found the chow coming in regularly, he stayed. The ingrate.

"Naturally, you can take him back," said the lady. "But he seems so happy here."

"What does he like to do?"

"We let him sleep on the mantel. He adores sleeping on the mantel."

We have no mantel.

What kind of cat is that? The cynical, conniving—well, I won't say it.

Of a whole litter of Siamese, Freddy was the one who was always in trouble. He got locked in cupboards. He had a roaring voice and complained constantly.

When the kittens were learning to drink milk out of the saucer, he was the one who stepped in it and upset it.

Do you think this gave him an unhappy childhood?

No, sir. His mother adored him. She polished and Simonized him twice as much as the other good little kittens.

That cat had it made. And he made the most of it.

When we gave all the other kittens away, we kept Freddy. The children were afraid the poor stumblebum could not get along in the world.

We kept him and lavished affection and canned cat food on him.

If he sniffled he got vitamins.

Nothing was too good for Freddy. And that is the way he felt about it, too.

Without turning a tap of work, without chasing a lizard, this cat led the life of a rich cat. All on my bounty.

And then, for the love of Pete, he has to move out and move in with people so he can sit on a mantel.

I have seen him on the mantel and he looks very decorative.

He knows it.

There is enough fresh breeze this morning that I must close the window. Summer is over.

We are making preparations for a birthday. A lively young man bent on taking the world apart.

"Did you have anything in mind?" said the saleslady.

"A child's bottle of Miltown?" I said hopefully.

"We'll try to find something constructive," she said. "A child needs the psychological reassurance of *doing* something. Let us think. What would that be?"

"A Boy Scout ax and five minutes alone with the hi-fi set,"

I said gloomily. "This child's idea of construction is to set off an atom bomb under the cat. I would not wish to bruise a tender psyche, yet there is a matter of self-preservation."

Well, we have many constructive toys for children these days. The cowboy outfit of my constructive youth has been changed considerably.

I remember that my cowboy outfit was a cap pistol and a beaded shirt.

There was a cowboy hat to go with it. Also an Indian war bonnet.

When you were a cowboy, you wore the cowboy hat and kept your shirt tucked in. When you wanted to be an Indian, you simply put on the feathers and pulled your shirt out so it hung outside.

The lady lifted two realistic .45s in tooled holsters. They were so realistic if she had pointed them at me I would have handed over my wallet.

"Exact replicas of the guns worn by Wyatt Earp on Channel 4," she said. "Or is it 5? They are balanced so that the child can do the 'Montana roll.'"

She spun the guns end over end to demonstrate.

"Suppose this child gets loose and points these over the counter at the corner piggy? They might tuck me away in the slammer as an accomplice."

"He would hardly be tall enough to reach the wicket. Ha, ha."

"This child climbs on chairs. Ha, ha. What else?"

"Here," said the lady, "we have a new educational toy called 'Custer's Last Stand.' It contains 80 action figures of soldiers and Indians. Made of unbreakable plastic.

"With the kit," she said, "goes a 16-page historical booklet. Outlining the battle. There is also a large lay-down map of the battlefield so that the action can be reconstructed."

"You mean we might win at last."

"If Reno advances and Custer does not split his command in the face of a superior force.

"Does he like books?" said the lady. "Some children take naturally to books."

"This child takes naturally to books. He takes them and just naturally pulls them to pieces. He has done more to the *Complete Works of Shakespeare* than the critics of the centuries."

"We have the *Book of Knowledge*—the children's encyclopedia. Suppose your child says: 'Can fish hear, Daddy?' "

"I would bust him in his little chops. No child is going to double-talk me."

"In this book you find the answer. It is a 20-volume mine of information with 7,600 delightful pages of pictures and inspiring articles."

"Do you have a cap pistol?" I said. "And a shirt you can tuck in or pull out?"

"I suppose so. What size?"

"About my size," I said. "So we can play together."

I have been doing a little pumpkin carving lately. In order to carve a proper jack-o'-lantern you must have a pumpkin, a dull knife and a small, attentive boy.

I learned my pumpkin-carving trade from a pumpkin-carving grandfather.

And he learned it from *his* grandfather. It is a family art.

"First we cut the eyes." That is what I tell my young son. "And be very, very careful with the knife. *Ouch!*"

That is why you should have a dull knife. One that just chops you lightly without lopping off your arm.

If I had used a sharp knife all these years, I would be all thumbs. No fingers.

We buy our pumpkins in the store. For some reason, nobody reminds me to plant pumpkin seeds during the summer and I have a lot on my mind.

I remember to plant pumpkin seeds about mid-October. Too late.

My grandfather said store pumpkins could not compare really with field pumpkins. He said the best time to pick them was a good, dark midnight.

His father had been a farmer. And when he moved to town, he thought the prices charged by other farmers were outrageous.

"Pa said it was all right to *borrow* a pumpkin," said my grandfather, whittling away, "so long as you didn't disturb the farmer and wake him up."

I have been unable to locate a field of pumpkins. Otherwise I would borrow one at midnight.

Grandpa said they cut better. Also they made better pumpkin pies. He didn't know why. Just knew that borrowed pumpkins were better than bought pumpkins.

Some people cut jagged teeth on their jack-o'-lanterns. But we cut a big, wide-open smile. Then we cut teeth separately and stick them in with toothpicks.

We leave a few gaps. A jack-o'-lantern should look a little like a small boy. A few teeth missing.

Some people leave the eyes blank. We cut the round end off a squash or a cucumber and stick those in the eyeholes. It gives the lantern green eyes. The eyes are propped forward so he looks popeyed.

When you cut the top off the pumpkin, you cut a wedge out of one edge.

This lets the candle smoke out. That is the theory. Actually it is the top of the pumpkin that gets hot and smokes. It smells a little for a while. But later it gets smoked up and you can close the windows again.

A pumpkin should be carved about three days before Halloween. It should be placed in the window each night. You can go out and look at it.

You can easily see it would scare anybody to death who walked up and looked at it. It even scares us a little. Not too much because we are brave. (We eat a breakfast food that makes us brave. Says so on the package.)

The pumpkin should be carved in the early evening. It should be a brisk, autumn day with a smoky sort of twilight.

The seeds should be taken out. We wash them and dry them. Then we put them in butter and salt and roast them in the oven. They are delicious.

Besides that, they are good for you. Make you braver than breakfast food.

They have medical value. If you grind your teeth at night, eat roasted pumpkin seeds and you will stop. I doubt if many doctors know that.

By following these rules, you will be healthy and brave. And your pumpkin will scare the wits out of the neighbors.

Borrow the pumpkin if possible. And don't wake up the farmer. He has had a hard day.

"Do you notice anything new?" she said anxiously.

"Are you doing your hair differently?"

"No. Can't you *see?*"

"The dog looks better," I said desperately. "The cat—now, wait a minute, I'll get it. Is it animal, vegetable or mineral?"

"I've got *high heels!*" she said.

"Why, of course," I said gaily. "I saw right away that you were looking more mature. 'What is it,' I said to myself, 'that makes this child resemble a more prominent movie star? What is it that has given her that mature look of a Woman Who Has Suffered?'

"It was so overwhelming," I said, "that I could not lower my eyes from the tragedy written on your brow to see the elegance of your tootsies."

"Stop!"

"Walk around a little," I suggested.

She walked around. Wobbly but it left me somewhat gloomy. Once they start walking around in high heels, they never give them up. After that we segue into the mink coats and heaven knows where it all ends.

The weather, as stated, is cold on our street. Frost lies under the redwoods when I go down to get the morning paper.

The dog walks down with me. Unhappily. He lifts his feet off the cold ground something like a fourteen-year-old girl in high heels. But not so impressed.

His idea of a satisfactory morning is to flake out by the fire. He grumbles about this walking down to the end of the road for the paper. But he comes anyway. He has a sense of duty about it but he thinks I am a fool.

The same old cat does the same old thing. She stays by the fire, scarcely opening an eye when I go out the door.

Well, there was a time when the dog could hardly wait to

get out into the chilly morning to get the papers. And I think I creaked a good deal less going up and down hill.

High heels have made a pretty doddering individual of me. It is like having young gentlemen come calling me "sir."

Anyway, we all went down to the neighborhood movies the other night. (We watch the movies pretty closely these days. Also the film magazines. We have firm convictions on movie stars and how they get married and divorced and all that, so we keep in touch.)

"I'm cold," she said.

"Just snuggle up beside me inside this coat," I said generously putting an arm about her. But she sat up and declared:

"Don't! Somebody might be watching!"

"For heaven's sake," I cried. "Surely a father is entitled to wrap his child in warmth and affection. You did not say such things at eight years.

"I am grown-up now," she said primly.

And I do not know which of us was chillier. Me in my warm coat or her in her warm convictions.

A blue-sky day with a snap in the air. The nights are colder and so are the mornings. Up in New England they are measuring the bands on striped caterpillars to see if it is going to be a hard winter.

This is done each year and is pretty silly, if you ask me. How would a caterpillar know if it is going to be a hard winter? When even the weather bureau has gotten so cagey it lays *odds* on the weather.

"Overcast with chance one out of ten of rain." That is the way they forecast these undetermined days.

Suppose a caterpillar *did* know it was going to be a hard winter. Why would he grow himself wider stripes? The caterpillar measurers are just confusing things.

It will be a hard winter. I have been measuring the stripes on my pajamas. The stripes are not getting wider. They are just fading. A sure-fire indication.

The other night the hot-water heater blew a gasket.

The house was knee-deep in hot water. The price of replacing this item is $190. Nobody has to tell me it will be a hard winter when you have to come up with a sudden One-nine-oh. Oh, oh.

I would like to know why heaters blow just three months after the guarantee runs out. Did you ever notice that? A guarantee is worse than a time bomb. I do not want a guarantee on my new heater.

If they give me one, I will soak it in a bucket of water.

At this season, you should get the popcorn popper out of the attic. And you should lay in a supply of nuts. Also some apples.

Buttered popcorn and salted nuts and apples are very sustaining in cold weather.

In these modern days, we have an electric popcorn popper. I am against most inventions, which are usually more bother than they are worth. But the popcorn popper is an improvement.

In my youth, I was named official popcorn popper. (In the summer I was official crank turner on the ice cream freezer.) We popped it on a stove. The popcorn was poured into a sheet-iron popper and then you shook it like crazy!

If you stopped shaking, the popcorn burned.

Your arm would ache and your back got sore. But you kept on shaking. You could not quit.

A lot of the popcorn burned anyway. But if you shook the bowl when you were buttering it, the burned kernels sank to the bottom. When we got to the bottom, we ate the kernels anyway. They were saltier.

Saltier, but noisier. When everybody was eating the kernels, it sounded like running a stick along a picket fence.

This is also fudge-making season. I am no fudge maker—that is women's work. But I am a great fudge beater. That is backbreaking work, too. You think your arm will drop off.

Like popcorn, you cannot stop. Or else everybody will holler, "Keep beating! Don't let it turn to sugar!"

I think nowadays we have instant fudge. You don't have to beat it. But we did not have instant fudge when I was a boy. We had instant boys. "Beat that fudge this instant!" That is what they told you.

Come to think of it, I do not think people could have faced the hard winters when I was a boy. Without boys. Boys do all that back-cracking work.

"Bring in the wood! Beat the fudge! Shake the popcorn!"

All this is done by machinery now. However, if the electricity goes off, we have a boy in reserve. And I am just the person who can tell him what to do and how to do it.

This boy has built-in ability. He is a pan licker. He licks fudge pans. And any boy that can lick a fudge pan, can beat, shake or crank. Winter cannot be too hard with that kind of talent around.

Once you have built a house, you must pass a "Building Inspection."

This was complete news to me. Heaven knows I had faced

a lot of things you do not dream of when you are dreaming of a family nest. "Title Search" was one.

"It is ridiculous to search for a title," I said. "I have made the down payment. And am into the World's Largest Bank for a mortgage that looks like an unfavorable trade balance."

Well, some people cannot understand logic.

I built the house. I cleared the title. I paid off the banker.

I put in a barbecue pit. I bought a foreign sports car and a leather-rimmed sports cap to go with it.

I passed the Building Inspection. There was talk of putting me up for membership in the Country Club.

By and by, we built a new room on the house.

"The building inspector is here!" The news is relayed by my teen-age daughter—over the plastic door into the privacy of my shower.

"Wrong house," I said. "Tell him."

"WHAT? I CAN'T HEAR YOU!"

"Tell him to go away. We have been inspected. We were inspected for termites and joists. For fireplace flues and good intentions. Go away!"

"HE SAYS IT IS FOR THE NEW ROOM."

"Good grief," I said. "You show him around, my dear. Point out the good points."

Oh, me. Oh, my. Telephones and building inspectors ring while I am in the shower.

This additional room, I might say, is for a very young boy. It is constructed of the finest materials. It looks like I imagine the cells looked in the Bastille.

Where ordinarily you put in two-by-fours, I put in four-by-fours.

Where plans called for aluminum doors, I put in tank-armor steel.

136

We screwed the iron bed to the floor and took his shoe-laces away. So he could not hang the cat.

"Let's see you wreck *that*," I said.

I must say he is trying.

"HE SAYS YOU HAVE NO STAIRS LEADING TO THE GROUND FROM THE BACK PORCH," she bellowed. "IT IS COUNTY CODE UMPTY-UMP."

"It is not a 'back porch,'" I said coldly. "It is a sun deck. Watch your language!"

"HE SAYS HOW DO YOU KEEP CHILDREN FROM FALLING OFF THE EDGE?"

"We nail his pants to the floor, tell him. We nail them to the floor and put him in them."

"WHAT IS THE HOLE IN THE GROUND? COUNTY CODE CLIPPETY-CLOP, HE SAYS."

"It is drainage. The water goes in there, 'round and 'round, and it comes out here—on the floor sometimes. Other times it backs up in the patio."

She went away for a while. I hoped she was giving the Inspector a cool bottle of beer. Or at least a cool line of chatter.

Drainage is a frightfully expensive thing. It cost me a fortune just to have that hole dug. I suspect they want me to put in drain tile. Poorhouseville.

"HE SAYS YOU NEED A RETAINING WALL ON THE BANK THAT IS SLIDING!"

"I need a wailing wall, tell him. Look—put on an old dress. Look poor."

"HE SAYS GET ALL THIS FIXED AND HE WILL SIGN THE PERMIT! COUNTY CODE NUMBER RICK-ETY-RACK."

"What else did he say?"

"HE SAYS THE ELECTRICAL INSPECTOR WILL BE
HERE THIS AFTERNOON."
"Oh."

Nothing would do but we must take the young squire downtown the other eve to get acquainted with Santa Claus.

It was a fine brisk night. There was a single star in the
sky and the store windows gave off great peals of Christmas
music. Electric trains ran in and out of tunnels. And rows
of dolls stared poker-faced at all us people on the sidewalk.

Santa Claus sat in the window—you could walk right in
and talk to him. He was wired for sound. Had a microphone
under the beard.

"Ho, ho, ho," he said electronically amplified. "And what
do you want for Christmas?"

The young squire peered at this man doubtfully. He got
behind my legs and peeked around. I don't blame him.

This is an emotional season. Especially tough on moppets.
All the grandmas had turned out to smile through tears as
little Joey met Santa Claus.

The thing is, little Joeys are not hep to Santa Claus the
first time around. Their eyes got big and they hung back
fearfully. No wonder.

For all they knew the big lug with the whiskers might *eat*
them.

I can imagine. Suppose you are raised in a quiet community. The men you see do not wear red suits and white
whiskers and talk metallically through a loudspeaker. How
do you know what a person like that will do?

Christmas, if you ask me, is for grandmas.

The grandmas were having the time of their lives. I will say that.

"Oooh," they cried. "Go up and see Santa Claus, Joey."

The Joeys burst into tears.

"I wanna go home!"

The mothers were mighty upset. "Go see Santa Claus," they hissed. "Grandma brought you down here, didn't she?"

The Joeys then put on a sullen and desperate look. They dragged up the ramp like a convict doing the short walk to the long stretch. They sat in Santa's lap dumbly. When they were released, they scuttled off.

You could see them figuring: "It will be a long, cold day before Grandma puts me in that spot again."

The four-year-olds had been through this wringer before. They were red hot to get to Santa Claus and a few of them went through the line twice—between times they cased the show windows and then went back to mention a few things they had forgotten.

"You want to see the nice Santa Claus?" I asked my own tot.

The young squire gave me a stricken look. Then he reacted the way small boys will react when faced with grave decisions.

Well, by and by we got him changed and headed for the toy department. I was born too soon. They did not make toys like this when I was a child.

I am no longer a child. But there is nothing wrong with trying out these toys, is there? I am not *playing* with them. I am testing.

Boy, oh boy! They have an army truck with a radar. You can make it move by blowing a certain note on a little whistle. The truck moves and the radar goes 'round and 'round!

I make the grandmas and mothers and other womenfolk hold the small fry when I am testing. The small fry screams like an eagle.

In a word, I would say visiting Santa Claus these days is well worth while. If you are a grandma. Or an expert at running toy trucks.

On the way out, we passed Santa again. The young squire shifted sides. So I was between him and the Santa Claus. He thinks I can lick him.

Since Christmas our street has been full of atomic scientists and burp-gun shooters. The toys of this year are made for mass mayhem rather than the single squirt-water pistols of my salad days.

For sheer ferocity, however, nobody has come up to the Eastman Kodak people who are making cameras so simple that even a child can operate one. And more's the pity, I say.

As a matter of fact, a child is operating one. I wish it were somebody else's child. But it is not.

"*Hold it.*" Flash, click!

"Heavenly days, child, at least wait until I get a towel around me." Also, I say, "It is unnerving to have a flash globe go off in your face in the early morning. Especially before coffee."

That is the trouble with these new cameras. A child can and does operate them. I have been flashed and pictured in such candid poses that I am secretly planning to destroy the film.

I do not remember any such vicious machines when I was a youth.

In my youth, I had a box Brownie. It was a black box and the black rippled paper on it had a tendency to peel and leave unattractive flaps. You pointed this at people and, if they held perfectly still in the bright sunlight, you often had a picture.

The Brownie presented this Christmas to my daughter is a precise instrument. The outside does not peel. It glimmers with chrome stripping. It has a fast shutter mechanism and a faster film.

It has a flash gun that blinds you at 50 feet.

It is the apple of her eye.

"Look this way." Flash, click! "That was a good one!"

"What was I doing?" I said nervously.

"You were scratching your back, so funny."

"What are you going to do with the pictures, my dear?"

"Oh, take them to school. And show them to people. You know."

"Look, could we make a deal. You could sell me the pictures. And the negative, too. Don't forget that."

"How much?"

"A dime a picture."

"Nope."

"Why not!"

"Because there are real George pictures on the roll. Oh, one's so funny when you were brushing your teeth and blowing, you know. So funny with all that goop on your chin."

"Fifteen cents," I said desperately.

"Nope. But I'll tell you what I'll do. You buy me five rolls of film and I'll give you this one."

"That's robbery!"

"Okay. If you don't want to—"

"It's a deal," I said hastily.

Well, I expect Mathew Brady would have been happy to have such a camera. When he was running around north Virginia and developing wet plates in the back of a wagon.

I think, though, we are carrying the camera too far. When we make it available to children. The box is getting too candid.

What really makes me mad though is that I have a camera myself. It is an intricate, beautiful German camera and I would no more tell you how much it cost me than I would let you see my child's pictures.

I have light meters to tell me how light it is. And focusing gadgets and distance estimators.

And what makes me furious is that most of my pictures come out fuzzy and out of focus. Even though it takes me half an hour to get ready. While that incredible Brownie, in the hands of a daffy child, gets sharp, clear beautiful pictures. Mostly of me in the most embarrassing furious moments. Why is that?

As an antique follower of the lonely hearts columns, I am happy to report that a whole new generation is taking up the torch.

The new generation, in fact, can hardly wait to have problems. And I find letters to "Dear Miss Lovelorn" all over the house.

> I like a boy who is much older than I am. He has asked
> me for a few dates but in order to keep a date I have to sneck

out of the house. He has asked me to elop with him. But I don't want to ruin my parents repitation. He told me that he has being married a few times. I don't know what to do.

HARD TO GET

This seems like a pretty fair problem. In fact a fairly alarming problem when applied to your own heiress.

"Who is this Lothario who is about to ruin my repitation?" I said gloomily.

"Not really," she said. "It's just a letter. Just to see what they answer."

"You mean you are writing letters to the lovelorn column? Regularly?"

"We all write letters. Do you want to see some?"

"I do indeed."

I should report that these letters are done in seventh-grade printing. Blue school ink on ruled theme paper.

DEAR MISS LOVELORN: My landlady was having some work done in the same hall I live. Onc day I was cobing my hair when the door opened and one of the workmen came into check the heater. I was about to tell him of when he told me not to mind him. He was very hanshom and next day he asked me for a date. I am now engaged to him. But he embassed almost all my friends. I don't know what to do. Please help.

"This incident, I trust, is imaginary? You have no secret landlady?"

"No, we just write the letters."

"And what does the lady answer in the columns?"

"She never answers," my lovelorn child said sadly. "But we write just the same."

Well, I am no man to go around telling other people how to write their columns. But I think this up-and-coming generation should get a few answers.

They have some pretty good problems. Just as good as the ones I see printed in the paper and signed "Mother of Six." Or "Unhappily Wed."

The fact that these girlish letters are a little unreal has nothing to do with the case. These are the problems they hope to have. And in the normal unhappy course of events, why not?

> DEAR MISS LOVELORN: I am a happly married wife of two children. But my husband nags a lot. He says things that I know he doesn't mean but I seems like I do everything wrong. Should I just let this ride or speck to him about it. Everything is a mess.

You cannot get much better problems than that. From a happily married wife of two children. Happily not.

I think this deserves a clear-cut answer.

So does this communication which I have read and given considerable thought:

> DEAR MISS LOVELORN: Every scince I was 7 I have taken care of my drunk dad. He is died now and I am married to a drunk husband. When I try to take care of him he just slaps me around. I am bewilded.
>
> BEWILDED

The weather has been wonderful. The more wonderful the weather, the more invitations to lunch. Have you noticed that?

On bad days, hardly anybody calls up and says: "How about lunch?"

But let the sun come out and the day get mellow. *Everybody* wants to get into a nice dark room and munch martinis.

I am having lunch this day with my young son and heir. We are on the right track. On nice days we eat *outdoors*.

I call him up on the play telephone.

"Pardon me, sir. Would you care to have lunch and talk over some important business?"

We agree to meet in one minute in the patio.

The menu today is peanut butter sandwiches. He wanted to add an Easter egg—heavenly days, I thought I counted them all, but we found a purple one behind the bookcase. It is pretty dusty.

We have agreed to use it for table decorations.

"Talk business, Daddy." Very well. This is a business lunch and you cannot start too early.

"My proposition, sir, is a proposition on toys. We are able to offer you a bag of six assorted colors of plastic autos for 59 cents. We will defer the payment of this amount for about a hundred years. Okay?"

It is agreed that I may deliver this shipment. It should come right after the nap. A very good business session, I should say. I have made a sale. He has made a good buy.

What did you do for lunch? I suppose you went in some dark, dismal place and got nowhere.

The Father-and-Son relationship is not easy. You have to be on your toes.

"Relationship between parent and child should be one of mutual trust."

That advice appears in a book on our shelves. It is for

parents—the child cannot read, naturally, and wouldn't trust you if he could.

The reason children do not trust you is because your stories are so unbelievable. For a week while the Easter baskets emptied, I swore that I could not bear chocolate Easter eggs.

"Daddy doesn't eat chocolate Easter eggs," was the cry around the scatter. "Rabbits don't eat chocolate Easter eggs."

This was supposed to tout the offspring onto more acceptable food. If your daddy hates chocolate Easter eggs and eats spinach; if the bunny rabbit hates chocolate Easter eggs and eats carrots—well, you get the idea.

This does not impress this child at all. He *likes* chocolate Easter eggs. And in his book, Daddy and the bunny rabbit lose plenty face. If they want to eat carrots and spinach, they can have *his* carrots and spinach.

He will take the chocolate eggs.

Anyway, he caught me nibbling a chocolate egg. I immediately put on a terrific act. Making a terrible face and clutching my chest.

"Oh, oh. How awful! I *hate* these nasty old chocolate eggs."

He gave me a doubtful look and said: "Give me a taste."

Secretly, if that child really switched off chocolate eggs to carrots, I would be pretty moody about it. He may be missing some vitamins. But he was not behind the door when the brains were passed out.

My mail this morning is a crisp pamphlet from Metropolitan Life Insurance. It invites me to "Understand Your Teen-Ager."

This I would surely like to do.

My teen-ager is fifteen. It is a curious age of slumber parties. Of bare feet, roasting marshmallow, sleeping bags and far-into-the-night conversations.

"He's the cookie with the wookie!"

I have been searching Metropolitan's booklet for a translation of this material. It is a pretty feeble effort. If Metropolitan wants me to understand a teen-ager, maybe they had better learn the language first.

"The teen-ager," says the Metropolitan, "will try to test your authority."

I suppose what they mean by this is these kids will spend hours trying on lipstick. And then scream like wounded eagles about washing down the bare feet before climbing into the sack.

This is not confined to *my* teen-ager. It is a thing that runs through the whole outfit. Marshmallow-smeared and goggle-eyed listening to Elvis Presley on the phonograph.

"He's the cookie with the wookie!"

"Ladies," I said, "kindly give a tottering old codger the word on this. What kind of cookie would that be?"

"It means just like that. He's *keen!* He drives a Nash with the pash!"

(Says Metropolitan: "The teen years are exciting and challenging years for the youngsters and for their parents too." All I can say is this is an interesting way of looking at it.)

I don't think Metropolitan came to grips with this thing at all. It is all pretty vague about how these kids feel. What about what they *do?*

I would like to know a few things, for instance. Why is it

when you send a child out to empty the garbage, you find them sitting there half an hour later?

"What are you doing?"

"Thinking."

"About what?"

"Just *thinking!*"

"Oh." (Once I found her waltzing barefoot with the garbage can in the garage.)

Or, how does it happen that a child with normal co-ordination can stand eating ice cream. And suddenly drop the plate on a brick floor right behind you?

"Great guns! What happened?"

"It just turned over in my hands. I had it with both hands and it turned."

These are things not contained in the sunny, sympathetic manual I read in the post office this morning. It does not contain information on why they will spend four hours in a bathtub one day. And must be throttled to comb their hair the next.

Or why a hang-jawed fifteen-year-old boy can cause hysterics in a whole covey of these females by merely walking by. To my mind, this youth is a candidate for the front and side-view pictures on the post-office wall. But to my slumber guests, he is the cookie with the wookie.

For the first time in a wary life, I am experimenting with an electric blanket.

For a long time I have been looking at those ads. You know, the ones where the husband and wife are sleeping at different temperatures? (It never says *what* temperatures but they both have smiles on their faces.)

I have looked at this happy couple in the slick magazines
and wondered. Haven't you?

Has she got her temperature turned down to Sun Valley?
While he lies there turned up to Tahiti? It is an interesting
thought. And I would like the ad men to tell me what they
lie a-dreaming of.

"On the coldest nights," said the salesman, "you sleep
under this blanket like a baby."

"I do not know whether I am flexible enough," I told him.
"When my children were babies, they slept on their knees.
Face down and with their back ends elevated. Such posi-
tions," I said, "would make me creak like an ungreased
wagon wheel. Don't you have a blanket that I can sleep
under like myself?"

"It is a figure of speech," he said. "You sleep well and
soundly. Warm as toast."

"Sometimes I do not want to be as warm as toast. Especially on summer nights."

"In that case, you may turn the New Night Watch Control
to a lower point. A small box which can be clipped to the
bedspring or placed conveniently on the night table."

Well, I am no match for a determined salesman. The
blanket arrived by delivery man. And though it was early,
I went to bed immediately and began to read the directions.
What complications!

"Congratulations," said the instruction book. "You now
own the Sleep-tite Automatic Blanket. The Finest Money
Can Buy."

It said I should switch on the control and a small light
would show under the dial. "Most people prefer dial-setting
at 4 or 5."

I set the dial to 4—no use frying myself—and lay down tensely.

The minute I lay down the light went off.

I looked at the instruction book again: "And don't forget —your blanket control adjusts automatically to temperature changes. You stay cozy warm."

I checked this out. It was a cold night and I was *not* cozy warm. My feet were like ice.

"If the light goes out, your blanket may sense overheating. Straighten out the blanket and reset the control by pushing the lever forward in the same manner as indicated in the above paragraph on how to Start Blanket."

That is a flowery paragraph. If I wrote like that, editors would sense overheating and straighten me out.

We straightened out the blanket. Flipped the switch two or three times. Nothing.

I lay down under the blanket and tried to get my feet warm by rubbing them on the sheet. Baby, it was cold outside!

The light came on again. Don't ask me why.

I put the switch up to 5. The light immediately went out.

I straightened the blanket again. The light went on. I crept under it cautiously. Not to disturb one tiny filament. Or let the blanket sense that I was even there.

The light went off.

I then got up and took a hot bath and put the old blankets on the bed.

And do you know, I slept like a baby. Got on my knees and slept face down. That way you can sit on your feet and be warm as toast.

Before Father's Day of this year is naught but a yellowed calendar leaf, let us record some minor history:

The first thing my son did on Father's Day was to point a small rubber pistol at me. "Bang!" he cried.

The first thing my daughter did was borrow a dollar. (It is a well-secured loan. Sound as Fort Knox. She will pay it back even if she has to borrow another dollar from me to do it.)

Father's Day is relatively new. It has never caught on with quite the enthusiasm that Mother's Day has.

For most of us, Father's Day is pretty much like any other Sunday. You don't go to work. And you either get pistoled or borrowed from. Maybe both.

It was a warm and sunny day. Nice smell of redwood and madrone off the hillside. Out where the hill slid during the winter rains, we found a treasure trove: a whole yellow-plastic rodeo of little horses and cowboys swinging ropes and such. We had almost forgotten we put them there.

We took them down on the brick patio and washed them with the hose. Good as new. While I set them up on the outside table, the small boy washed his pants and shoes with the hose.

He had the pants and shoes on at the time.

It was an interesting idea and, I imagine, pretty cooling. We changed the pants and shoes.

I was invited to look over a number of improvements and repairs that are contemplated for the old homestead. They will cost a fortune. But I am a fortunate man.

It was stated that nobody wanted to ruin my Father's Day. But—"It's Sunday and when else are you home to see these things for yourself? Like that window where the rain got at it. That *has* to be replaced."

The whole hillside slid right off the hill during the winter rains. It slid right into the back yard.

Personally, I think this pile of earth adds a rustic feeling to the place. I would leave it alone. Let it grow a fine fringe of grass. Why, when I was a boy, I would have given anything for a little hillslide like that.

It has roots of trees tangled up in it. You could build a terrific fort and fight Indians from behind it. You could gallop over its small horizon and rescue the ranchers.

A slide like that was put there by providence. It would cost a small fortune to get such a thing in your yard. And here we got it for nothing.

Well, it seems that this slide upsets the geometric mind of a formal gardener.

It also interferes with drainage.

We have a curious drainage problem. Mostly water runs downhill, as every school child knows. I wish the teacher would come out to my house.

At my house all the water runs uphill! This is an unexplained, scientific fact. Any old rain water we have around runs right uphill and then stands around in the yard. It likes it in my yard, I guess.

Anyway, water will not drain. Even though we live on the edge of a 45-degree slope. We have to install cunning little drainpipes and dig enormous ditches to keep it moving.

It moves sluggishly and reluctantly. Where it stands still, the house rots away. If I told you how expensive it is to coax water to drain, you would not believe it.

For Father's Day, I was presented with wallet-sized pictures of my children. My daughter paid for them out of her baby-sitting money. They look very handsome. She can borrow a dollar any time she wants to.

I am informed that we have a new school newspaper. This paper, like all good journals, is dedicated to high ideals. Like gossip. And what boy likes what girl. And editorials demanding school spirit.

My own young lady has been appointed to write a column. (You know how it is—the piano player's daughter should sit down at the piano. That's logic.)

"But I can't think of anything to write," she cried.

Well, my heart bleeds for this embryo journalist. It truly does.

"It is probably something that runs in the family," I said dejectedly. "For to tell the truth, your father is often cursed with the same emptiness of thought. Have you tried?"

"I tried and tried. Would you like to see it?"

"Love it."

The column I find is labeled FIRST IDEA.

"An odd title. Where did you get it?"

"Because it was my first idea."

"Oh."

FIRST IDEA: What can teacher do when we get out of hand? We are to old for spanking and we are to young to have the privilege of not driving the car for a week.

If I were teacher I would lay down the law. They do something wrong and half an hour more of the ten Christian social principles.

"What do you think of it?" she asked.

"Well, it is short and punchy," I said cautiously. "Also it has some social principles. The problem is that it will not fill a whole column. That is always the problem."

"I have more," she said handing me the paper.

> SECOND IDEA: The opea called Madam Butterfly is now on Broadway. I don't think I have ever head such exciment since summer vacation was on its way. Up and down the domatories wabbling the girls walk in they first high heels. Then they run down stairs call their fathers oh daddy I saw the cutest dress and then it settled . . .

"Is that good?"

"It sort of goes off into nothing, doesn't it?" I said. "Settled what?"

"I forget because just then the bell rang. What else should I say?"

"Just write down the words. What you are doing. What everybody is doing."

"They aren't doing *anything*. I thought and thought."

"This is something I have discovered myself, my dear. You are not flagging me any new information."

I am informed that this piece must go into the paper next week. A deadline that hangs over our heads like a sharp sword. We are waiting for somebody to do something. Anything.

I have just read THIRD IDEA:

> Seems like this paper is coming out Okay. They have sports, society, liturature, advertising and a juicy lovelorn column.

I recognize this "paper is coming out okay" as a brave conjuring fling at the arts. It is not coming out okay. But maybe saying it will make it so. I have done the same thing myself.

We now come to the FOURTH IDEA. The Fourth Idea is conveyed to me in direct conversation.

"What I thought—well, you know it's so hard and you know *how* to do it. Anyway, what I thought was—well, you take my First Idea and kind of write the rest of it. Will you, please, please?"

That is what I sort of thought all these ideas were leading to. I could feel it coming. We now come to my First and Final Idea. Which is, no. I don't know anything, not a thing, about little girls "wabbling in the domatories in their first high heels."

I am a heel myself. I don't intend to find out.

Post-haste from Philadelphia today, Patent No. 2,822,717 has been issued to Mike Slawienski: An automatic beater for bass drums.

"After plugging the connection into the house current, the drummer can set the machine to execute a series of slow single beats or of faster double beats."

You want to know why? "It leaves the musician's hands and feet free for other instruments."

Nearly everything plugs into the house current these days —including the child's fingers if you do not watch him. If he did plug his fingers in I have often wondered what would come out. Hi-fi, maybe?

I plug into the house current and the TV screen comes alive.

"Reach for yore six-gun, varmint! On accounta how Ah'm gunna blast yuh, varmint!" Bang! Bang!

In the morning I can plug into AM, FM, or the electric shaver. Simultaneously if I like. My beard is chopped to "Who's gonna call you sweetheartttttt, if you call the whole thing offffffff . . ."

We plug into the house current and the genie sucks away the dust and the bobby pins into the mystic black bag.

Plug in and the house current beats the pancake batter. It turns on the sprinkler and runs the kitchen clock.

No wonder the light company can afford such haughtiness: "If this account is not paid within 10 days, we will be forced to . . ."

The man at the other end of the plug-in is master of our destinies.

Turn off the juice and we all stop. Like the frozen figures of the frozen castle, awaiting the Prince to come and dislodge the magic apple from the Princess' throat. (I kiss the magic light company with a magic check each first of the month. It keeps my castle plugged in and lively.)

No matter how well you plan your house, no matter how cunning the architect, the floor plug is always behind the couch. Did you ever notice that?

When we plug in the cleaner, I must push the couch out of the way and bend way over. Coming up I hit my head on the end table. (However, I once found a quarter back there so I am not complaining. My daughter raised the roof, claiming it was hers. But I beat her out of it. Children should not be spoiled with too much money.)

Some plugs are unpredictable. They sparkle and snap at you. There is a lot of smoke and blue flashes. Then all the lights in the house go out. This is the time when you appreciate what the man at the other end of the plug has been doing for you all these years.

You must take a flashlight—the batteries are usually worn down to a faint yellow glow. You take the flashlight out to the garage. And you screw in a new fuse.

Presto! The house lights up. The washing machine begins churning again. The icebox begins to hum. The clock begins to run. The stove goes on and the roast begins roasting.

There are hardly enough plugs to go around in a modern house. We pop corn by plug. Ironing is the direct result of plug to iron. We plug in the waffle maker and the electric fryer.

We plug in the plug that makes the water tropical for the tropical fish. When the winter storms cut the electricity, I lost a freezerful of frozen salmon and the tropical fish had to put on overcoats. There is a paradox for you.

Matter of fact, possibly a monument should be built to the plug. An enormous plug, carved in granite on Mount Rushmore. Beating drums, popping corn, freezing fish, warming fish.

There is no end to our plug-in life. Even at night. We plug in the electric blanket; the electric pad for my aching back. And so to plug-in dreams.

Do you know how to build a tree house? It seems to me I knew once. You nailed two-by-fours and planks up in the limbs.

I knew how to do it. But seem to have lost the knack. Nowadays I prop the family mansion with mortgages.

"Wouldn't you rather have a fort, son?"

I am trying to tout my offspring onto a fort. A fort requires no structural ability. Just throw together some breastworks of old apple boxes. You get down behind them with the old Daisy air rifle, cool as you please.

Here comes the pesky redskins! Bang! Bang! Take that!

Well, as long as I keep talking, my boy is with me. His eyes shine while I tell him how much *better* a fort is.

"Then you can ride for help to the nearest cavalry post," I told him. "Go! I will hold off the Sioux. You're too young to die and it does not matter about me, the Old Trapper."

And I wiped a tear from my eye to show him I did not mind dying at all.

It was a pretty good performance if I do say so myself.

"Build tree house, Daddy."

Now what can you do with a one-track child like that? The point is, I do not know how to build a tree house. But I am not copping to the younger generation.

It is a terrible thing to have your children find you out. I wish to stave it off as long as I can.

It seems some able father in our neighborhood—gad, how I hate these people who can saw and hammer—just went out one day with a few boards. And he built his son a tree house.

I am expected to do the same.

I have plenty of trees. But no talent.

"How about a nice trench?" I said desperately. "A trench is where soldiers fight. It is more fun than a tree house. Or even the zoo or a merry-go-round."

When I was a sprout of this age, we dug miles of trenches. We crouched in our trenches and fired over the top.

We shook hands with each other solemnly. We assured each other that we were too young to die.

In fact, we got into some bitter fights about *who* was allowed to die.

The boy who died would leap out of the trench and charge the enemy. He did it to save the rest of the company from sure annihilation. He charged while we stood by enviously. Then he fell and writhed beautifully and died.

That was what caused the fights. "Stay here, men! You are too young to die!"

"You died the last time! It's my turn now," we hollered.

If my boy would get off the tree-house thing, I would let him charge and die every time.

I am too old to die. Too old to charge, too. I would direct him how to dig the trench. Then I would sit in it, peering sternly over the top. I would not charge. I would wait for the enemy to come to me.

"Trenches are the very best thing and you can be the bravest soldier."

"Build a tree house, Daddy."

That boy will probably become a lawyer. He will not let go.

We have got a lot of boards and a lot of trees. And a man who cannot hang a picture without banging his thumb.

I cannot find a blueprint on a tree house anywhere. And have no idea how to go about it. Surely they must put out books on these things.

It looks like I will have to build a tree house the only way I know how. Down to the bank for a mortgage. An architect, a builder and a downstairs powder room.

Because if my son finds out how little talent I have, I will simply die. And I am too young to die. Charge!

Being in temporary possession of a jelly tot around the scatter, I have been making a study of the language. Shedding my freepy ways and learning to be a hipster.

If you do not dig me, Daddy-O, a jelly tot is like a Jim Dandy. Only younger. A Jim Dandy is a cool, cat-dopey kitten. Shall I increase the volume?

"Now that you are a jelly tot, which is to say a teen-ager, I shall converse with you in your native tongue," I said. "In later years, I wish you to gather your grandchildren about your bony knee and declare: 'Daddy-O learned a whole new language so he could talk to me.'"

"Gosh!"

"For instance," I said. "We will no longer go down to the drive-in and spend a dollar on hot dogs. We will hop in the container and blaze down to the drag-and-eat pad where I will unload a Chlorophyl George while we buzz around the barrel."

"Can we buy an Elvis Presley record?"

"A very eepy idea. In a word, mar-velvis. However, the word 'record' is not cultured. In fact, it is rather glunky. The word you are reaching for is 'CUTTINGS.' Shall we make like a tree and leave?"

"Where did you learn all that?"

"I am a cool Jonah," I said modestly, buffing my nails on my lapel. "In a way of speaking—and heaven knows a difficult one—your Daddy-O is a hubcap. Likewise hip. For we no longer use hep. A word belonging to the Dark Ages of 1955.

"I would not take on an entire language for any kitten," I said. "But being your parent, I purr for you."

"Talk some more," she said. "It's real neat."

"Neat is hardly the word for it," I said coolly. "It is zoolie. Enough to make you flip your wig. Shall we wind up the box and get some platter-chatter?"

"Does that mean play some records?"

"It does," I said. "Though the way you express it is rather gishy. It is the kind of language used by a cube. Which is a square in 3-D. People would think I did not send you to an expensive slaughterhouse if you talk like that. What does the riot squad teach you, anyway?"

"You mean school?"

"That is the way we cool cats say it. Get frantic. Don't you dig me? Don't be a pump, frump."

"I want to learn to talk like that," she said.

"Jelly tot," I said, "you have come to the right tiger. I am droolin' with schoolin'."

Not to change the channel, but I found the language not too difficult. If I can do it, you can do it. And, cats, if you have a teen-ager about the house, you must learn to communicate.

As a matter of fact, it is a good idea to stay a little ahead. For if you goof your lines, it is extremely freepy—a cross between a freak and a creep.

"As a starter," I told the jelly tot, "when speaking of your father to the other little jelly tots, you will declare: 'He's a rootin' tootin' Fig Newton.' This is complimentary and respectful.

"Of the way I dress, you may say I'm the iviest. You will speak of our dog as the fur piece. Your shoes will become your stompers, money will be bread and when you eat, you grease. The menu, by the way, will be referred to as the prescription. Do you dig?"

"Yes, Daddy-O. You're the lushest."

"Ice it, jelly tot," I said bashfully. "It's only static in the attic."

I haven't thought of it for years, son. But at one time your father came close to mastering the Indian rope trick.

I read about this wonderful thing in a youth magazine. A magazine with high ideals and the most fascinating ads. The ad said I could learn the trick absolutely free. But when I sent away for the information, it turned out they only told you free *what* happened.

They didn't tell you *how*. To learn how, you had to pay the postman $3.98 on delivery.

I do not remember how many hours I spent in the back yard, casting a rope into the air. Dressed in my underwear with a towel around my head. I never made the rope stand up so I could climb it. But small boys came from blocks around to watch. It was an interesting time of my life.

Well, what recalls these memories is fresh news from India.

Professor C. T. N. Singh is head of the botany department at Annamalai University. Miss Stella Ponniah is a musicologist. She plays the veena, which is something like a guitar.

This sounds like a romantic setting. But not so.

When Miss Ponniah hits the hot licks on the veena, she does not play for the Prof. She plays for his plants.

The plants go crrrrrrazy, man. Immediately they begin putting out new roots and leafing out.

The Professor subjected a Mimosa Pudica to Indian violin music for 25 minutes a day. While Mimosa Pudica without music grew 100 per cent, the Mimosa with the jive shot up 200 per cent.

The Professor set out some balsam seedlings. He set Miss Ponniah to work on the veena. The balsam with the bongo treatment picked up 72 per cent more leaf production than the balsams who just sat around and watched *Dragnet*.

This is so interesting that I have been playing my guitar at the Ranchipur lime tree. A Ranchipur lime is about the handiest thing you can have around a house.

It looks like an orange but tastes like a lemon.

The best thing about it is the peel. The peel is wonderful for wringing out over a dry martini.

I will report that this lime tree is not doing too well.

For a long time I have been doctoring this tree with left-over martinis. If anybody leaves any in the glass, I pour it on the lime tree. The tree does not get much. People are selfish and do not leave much martini in the glass.

It is my idea now to stimulate this lime tree with music. The Professor does not say what Miss Ponniah plays on the veena. But I imagine it is something like "Moonlight on the Ganges."

I play my lime tree 100 per cent American music.

I play it "The Night Before They Stretched O'Leary." I play it "They Tried to Tell Us We're Too Young." And "Love Is a Many-Splendored Thing."

I put in little trills and some very zoomy sliding notes. This lime tree gets my best talent.

I play for it best with a martini alongside—a little for me, a little for the lime tree.

It seems to me sometimes I can see this lime tree perking up. Sort of tapping its foot. It could be my imagination but I think this lime tree feels better. Its leaves look shinier.

With a little chilled martini and the strings humming. Both of us having a ball.

Our four-year-old son grows amazingly. He is about 6 feet tall. Maybe a few inches over.

First thing I do when I get home from long trips is to measure him.

I am amazed. Positively flabbergasted.

I back him up against the wall—it is a wall where we make pencil marks to show how tall he is getting. We make the mark, the new mark. We look at it and, heavenly days, he has grown another foot!

"You mean you *grew* that much while I was gone?"

He is delighted with his progress. In order to make the last mark, I put my elbow on his head and then made the mark. It was way up *there!*

If possible, he meets me at the airport. Being a child who takes things apart, he is very anxious to see what I have taken apart on an airplane. What I take apart is the soap dispenser. He likes to get small bars of soap.

That is not the opener, though. We have a routine.

He comes down the ramp yelling, "Daddy!"

"I beg your pardon, sir. I do not recognize you. Who are you?"

This is pretty good comedy. He has grown so much,

changed so much, that his own father does not recognize him! He then tells me who he is.

"No!" I drop my bags in amazement. (I dropped one on a lady's toe once, I am that good when the actor comes out in me. She was amazed. Sore, too.)

"Yes. I am."

"No. Impossible. Why when I went away, you were just a *little* boy. How did you grow up so fast? Did you eat all your cereal?"

Well, finally, he convinces me that he is really and truly the same boy I left.

Then we go home and I measure him against the wall.

We are amazed all over again and it is the finest reunion you could hope for. Imagine going away and leaving a small boy. And coming back and finding a boy 6 feet tall—if you measure him and make the mark by putting your elbow on his head. That and standing him on a small stool.

Naturally, we have a good many things to talk over. He likes to talk about the good old days. We have some good laughs over what he used to do when he was small.

The cat has scratched him. But it is nothing. Hardly enough for a Purple Heart.

This is a neighbor's cat who comes to visit. He carries the cat around like a sack of flour. Sometimes the cat objects.

"Did you pull the cat's tail, son?"

"No. Remember, I used to pull his tail. That was when I was a *little* boy."

"Those were the good old days, weren't they, son?"

We like to talk about those old days. Things are not as lively nowadays.

(The cat has not forgotten those good old days. About a month ago. When our child approaches with a rake or baseball bat, that cat goes right up a tree. The boy has an experimental mind. He is likely to try to clout the cat into left field.)

"What did you do while I was away? Tell me everything you did. Good or bad."

Well, he went to the zoo. He threw a rock at the bear.

"Did you hit him?"

No. But he almost hit him. It was a bad bear. Did you know there were good bears and bad bears? Bad bears eat you. But good bears make toys for Santa Claus. Fact.

"And then I grew up from a little boy into a big boy."

We go over and measure him again. Heavenly days, he has grown a full inch while I was talking to him: You can see the new pencil mark on the wall, if you don't believe me.

Life is not so simple, Daddy-O. Whud-uh, whud-uh. We are learning to drive the car these days. One hand for the steering wheel, one to punch the push buttons on the radio.

My heart beats to Sal Mineo singing "Little Pigeon."

My nerves throb to "Bop-a-Lena." Bop music, I find, is full of "whud-uh, whud-uh."

"*Got patent leather shoes—whud-uh, whud-uh—on my hound dog feet—whud-uh, whud-uh.*"

"WATCH THE CAR!"

"Yes, Daddy." Snap the button. "*Got those grown-up blues, whud-uh, whud-uh.*"

We go sailing down the back roads. The ducks are flaked out in the green, green spring grass. The sun is shining and the sky is blue silk.

The radio plays today's love songs: "*Sweet li'l sixteen—*

*whud-uh, whud-uh—way down in New Orleans—whud-uh,
whud-uh."*

The white sheep are on the hillside. The orange road
machinery is on the roadside. *"I'm on your side—whud-uh,
whud-uh. Are you on my side? Whud-uh, whud-uh."*

"Does my driving make you nervous, Pops?"

"Not at all, at all," I said.

"You're lighting the wrong end of your cigarette," she said
critically.

"Never mind my cigarette," I said. "Watch the road. I like
to smoke the filter first. The rest of the cigarette is for dessert."

Everybody must learn to drive, I suppose. But.

"Why do you press the pedal like that downhill?"

"It makes the car pop, Pops."

"Do not make the car pop. Drive the car. My nerves will
do all the popping necessary around here. Could we have the
radio just a little softer?"

"Yes, Father."

The car radio seems to have an automatic gain. It grows
louder and louder. The way you do this, each time you
push the push button, you just let your hand graze over the
volume knob. Turn it up just a little, little bit.

Do this often enough and you get it the way we like it.

"Who wears short shorts? Whud-uh, whud-uh. WE WEAR
SHORT SHORTS! WHUD-UH, WHUD-UH."

"Turn it down!"

". . . short shorts, whud-uh . . ."

"Isn't it a wonderful day," she said breathing deeply and
closing her eyes.

"Open your eyes. Speak to me," I said, grabbing the wheel.

"I am being very careful."

"Thank you. Those are pleasant words. I hope the words are close to your thoughts."

We cannot be too careful. When spring is in the air and the air is full of bop.

We turn into a gravel road and baaaaack around for the return trip. It is a wonderful day. The first golden poppies are coming up. You cannot beat such a day.

"Shall we have some more music, Pops?"

"There is nothing I would prefer more," I said. "To be driven through the countryside by my daughter to the strains of 'Cherry Pie.'"

My driving daughter agrees with me. Snap.

What a great day! *"Lollipop, lolli, lollipop. Whud-uh, whud-uh."*

7.

To lunch today at Moriarty's Chop House, the Sixth
Avenue home of the *bons vivants* of the New York press.

It was a wonderful day. New York is in between summer
and fall—neither topcoat nor shirt-sleeve weather. The fountains throwing up great sprays of sunlit water in Rocke-
feller Center. The brisk flow of walkers on Fifth Avenue and
bright flags blowing in the breeze.

"Do we have any relatives in Ireland?" My child and I
are en route to Ireland. I thought Moriarty's was an ap-
propriate beginning.

"Naturally," I said. "Who was it but me grand grandmother O'Dooleyplane who sang me to sleep to the tune of
'The Night Before They Stretched O'Leary'?"

"You aren't telling the truth, are you?"

There was a time when children had respect for their
elders. When the fact that I was the sole survivor of the

Custer massacre was not questioned. But now she is fifteen. A skeptic.

We are taking a pre-school vacation. It is an education for both of us.

I am learning that a fifteen-year-old girl can dress for dinner. And five minutes later completely shed her clothing when she is suddenly struck with the idea that what she had put on looks *terrible.*

"It does not look terrible. It looked fine to me. We are getting terribly late for dinner."

"It does so look *awful.* I haven't a thing to wear."

"My dear," I said, "the closet is bursting with clothes."

"None of them are any good. They aren't sophisticated."

That is the big idea these days—sophistication.

We spent two solid hours in a gown salon this afternoon. In and out of dressing rooms. My fingers are numb from hooking people up the back. In fact, I think I should get a small salary from the management.

There was an agony of choice. A very elegant brown dress was discarded as: "It looks like a little child's dress."

We tried on three times a beige thing called a "figure flatterer."

Once the saleslady actually had a dress packaged and the sales slip made out. But at this moment, a horrid doubt arose and it came out of the tissue paper while we tried on something else.

We finally got away with a thing in fire-engine red. It had been tried on in front of every mirror in the hotel. At intervals great moans come from the next room. I am sought out for desperate advice.

"Is it *really* grown-up looking?"

"It makes you look terribly old."

"How old?"

"At least seventeen. Ancient."

"I wish I'd taken the other one. I'll *never* look grown-up."

I got this girl a passport and a small quantity of travelers' checks. So she could learn. Learn to take care of things while traveling. So far I am getting all the education.

"I've lost the travelers' checks!"

"Then you will have nothing to spend," I said firmly. "That was what we agreed. You will have to get your money back from the bank."

"But I've lost my passport, too."

"No! We cannot leave the country without your passport. Did you look in your purse?"

"I've looked everywhere. I just lost it, that's all. It is your fault," she said with female logic. "You should have kept it for me."

We finally found the passport. And the travelers' checks. They were in the bathroom. Behind the shampoo. How they got there or why they got there, nobody seems to know.

I have learned quite a bit on this educational trip. Nearly everything gets lost. But it nearly always turns up again. Nearly always in the bathroom.

A drizzling rain was falling on New York when we drove out to Idlewild to board the night flight to Shannon, Ireland.

"I am hungry," she announced.

Well, this is no surprise. Yet it always astounds me. My daughter is slim and healthy. Yet she puts away groceries in a way to embarrass me. I am sure people think I starve her.

"You had a huge steak last night," I said. "And you had

an enormous steak sandwich for lunch. What do you want?"

"Another steak," she said.

We rolled down the gray strip and rose into gray skies. No sooner did the seat belts sign go off than the steward was around to put on the dinner action.

"I had a late lunch and will pass," I said. "Ouch!"

"I beg your pardon?"

"Nothing," I said, rubbing my ankle where my child had kicked me. She was pretending to read a movie magazine and giving me sidelong looks.

"We are proud of our dinners," he said. "You must eat."

"I don't care how proud you are. I'm not hungry."

"Order it anyway," my child hissed at me. "I'll eat it."

"I will take the dinner," I said gloomily. "My appetite has returned."

The steward went away. "I thought you were on a diet," I said.

"I'm starving," she said. The steward came back with the trays.

"Now," he said, "aren't you happy you ordered after all?"

Eating two dinners calls for a good deal of finesse. In the first place, *nobody* must *ever* know that you ate two dinners.

She polished off the meat course and changed to my full plate quickly and furtively.

"Pretend like you're eating," she hissed.

"I don't even feel like pretending to eat."

"Pretend anyway. Otherwise he'll know."

"What do you care if he knows? The company is not going to charge you just for gobbling two dinners. What about that diet, by the way?"

"I can't diet when it's so good," she sighed. "I will diet tomorrow. At least pick up your fork and pretend."

Everybody traveling with a growing girl should carry emergency rations. That is my advice.

There is nothing like going on a diet to stimulate the appetite.

I never thought a diet was needed. But it seems all teen-agers go on diets. The diet goes like this: First you get yourself a book that tells you how many calories are in everything.

Then you eat just as much as you ever did. Only you look it up in the calorie book first. When you read how many calories there are, you just *die*.

You die. But you go right on eating. Your own dinner and your father's. Looking up calories makes you fiercely hungry.

She finally settled down to sleep. And when we woke in the morning, the sun was up and the sky below was full of fat, white clouds. Little patches of blue sea came up below us and drifted astern and out of sight.

She opened one sleepy eye.

"When is breakfast?" she said.

I ate mine in a hurry. She giving me pitiful and starving looks all the time. Even though she ate hers first and got half of my roll when I wasn't looking.

We drove up to Dublin on a clear Irish day. The fields are washed grass-green and the Shannon mirrors the white, fluffy clouds.

We are driving a pint-size British Austin. The names of parts of the car convulse my teen-age child. The glove compartment is "the cubby locker"—a more likely title, to my thinking. Who keeps gloves in it anyway?

The hood is "the bonnet." The steering wheel is on the

right and you drive on the left-hand side of the road. (When I remember it.)

"Petrol, sir?" said the man in the service station.

"What's that?" she whispered.

"Gasoline. They call it petrol here."

"Omigosh!" What a wonderful world!

All Ireland is soaking in the rainiest rains in many years. The Dublin papers this morning show pictures inside Kilkenny Abbey Church—four feet deep in water. But—

It has not rained on us once!

This is a major disaster. I bought my daughter a new raincoat in New York. I assured her it rains somewhere every day in Ireland. That is my experience anyway. I am like a sponge in Ireland.

"You promised it would rain!"

"My dear, I still promise you it will rain. Though heaven knows I am not Jove. Hurling around thunderbolts and such. It says here in the paper it is raining. Raining *and* flooding."

"I think they make things up in the newspapers."

Scratch a journalist's child and find a cynic.

This morning in Dublin I pulled the curtains and looked into gray, damp skies. I got the cynic on the intercom. "Look out the window." Wow!

To Jammet's with its polished brass antique stairways for lunch. And waited on by gray-haired Jimmie Beggan in his elegant tail coat.

The menu is in French. For the original Jammet was brought from Paris to cook for the English Lord Lieutenant of Ireland. It is the best of Dublin restaurants, drawing marvels out of the tasty Irish beef and the wonderful Irish brown bread and butter.

Afterwards we shopped in fashionable Grafton Street. Walking up toward St. Stephen's Green.

"I've got to buy some grips," she said.

"No more baggage," I said firmly. "We are overweight right now. I have no intention of making the airlines richer than they are."

"Grips," she said. "That's what they call bobby pins here."

We learn a little more each day. Though the street signs in Gaelic are a stopper. Fortunately, most of them have the English translation underneath.

"Don't be bold," says the Irish mother to her child. Meaning: "Don't get fresh."

My daughter sent out her laundry today. "Is it Miss or Mrs.?" said the maid. Such possibility of looking older simply makes a fifteen-year-old flip. "Miss or Mrs?"

This morning I stopped to buy a paper while she went up ahead of me in the lift (that's an elevator, kids).

The lift boy is about fourteen.

"Your sister's already gone up, sir," he said when I came around.

"Don't be bold," I said.

But I gave him a shilling. Sister indeed. I went right up and looked at myself in the mirror in a pleased sort of way. Holding up very well. Very well.

From Dublin to Galway on the twisty Irish roads. Me in my fine, green linen waistcoat that I bought in Grafton Street.

My traveling companion looks gloomily on my elegance.

"Oh, please, please don't wear it! People will think we're tourists."

"A fine criticism from a girl who wears sack dresses," I said sharply. "It proclaims my independence and—if I do say so myself—is one of the sharpest weskits I have ever seen.

"Green linen," I said, "brings out the Irish in me. For who was it but me own grandmother O'Dooleyplane sang me to sleep! She wiped the froth of Guinness stout from her dear lips," I said, "and sang:

> *"Oh Paddy, dear, and did you hear*
> *The news that's goin' round?*
> *They're hangin' men and women*
> *For the wearin' of the Green."*

"You just look terrible," said my friend and severest critic.

However, I am a tiger when I have my mind set on a piece of clothing. I will not be intimidated.

We have run into "the travelin' people." A raggedy bunch with great round-covered wagons. Some people here say they are true Gypsies; others say they are pure Irish who have traveled the roads for generations.

"Tinkers, they call them," I said. "They trade horses and they mend pots. Just like Gypsies. Mothers scold their children in Ireland by saying: 'You're no better but a tinker.'

"Therefore, Irish children grow up politely," I said, "and do not criticize their father's fine green weskit."

The travelin' people give you a great shout as you drive by. My child had a dream about them the other night. (I am regaled with the night's dream each morning. And, believe me, if I wrote like this moppet dreams, our cupboards would soon be bare.)

"I dreamed I was kidnaped by the traveling people. And then I got away and went home. And my mother didn't recognize me. And my brother didn't recognize me. It was *horrible*. And then they did recognize me."

"Then what happened? I am on edge!"

"That's all. That was the end of the dream."

That is a pretty poor dream, in my estimation. I simply repeat it to show the kind of conversation I must put up with. A man in a green waistcoat who could probably command the finest conversations in Europe.

We have long conversations about how soon I will die. Heavenly days, what a life!

It seems I am going to cash in my chips soon—I am given a cheerful year or two. "When you die will you give me your gray sweater?" Things like that.

"My dear," I said, "I am in the rosiest of health and a broth of a boy. I intend to live for a long, long time and wear my gray sweater. And my green weskit."

"You are pretty old," she doubtfully.

"I am in my prime. I may join up with the travelin' people and go from town to town in a gay sort of way. Mending pots and kidnaping children."

"You look kind of green," she said.

So that's what we are getting at. I am being worked out of my green linen waistcoat. Sharper than a serpent's tooth is an ungrateful child.

But sharper than a razor blade is my fine green waistcoat. And so we drove over to Galway. In a conversational sort of way.

This is one of those days. We are in Paris. In stages. At the great, stone Hotel Crillon overlooking the fountains of the Place de la Concorde.

Our teen-age daughter follows from Ireland.

"Wake me at three in the morning," I told the maid.

"*Soyez tranquille,*" she said. "Be tranquil. Everything is arranged."

Each day my maid advises me to be tranquil. She is like a doctor with a bedside manner. "*Soyez tranquille, m'sieu!*" Come down off that chandelier.

Somebody knocked on my door at 6 A.M. and I picked up the phone. No answer. I jiggled the hook. This was a terrible mistake. No French phone is tranquil. And if you jiggle the hook, you send it into fits.

I got up and put on my clothes and went downstairs. I got a phone and called the airline.

"What time does your Flight 472 arrive?"

"It is late. It will not be in until 9:45."

I went back upstairs and got back in bed. I left word to call me at 8.

"*Soyez tranquille!*" said the night concierge.

At 8 o'clock the phone rang. I held onto the operator until I got the airline again.

"Is your Flight 472 still coming at 9:45?"

"The flight is now early. It is on the ground."

I called Orly and told the passenger agent to get hold of a sleepy-looking teen-age child and have her call me. Also please put her in a taxi. Get her money changed and tip the porters.

I got up and splashed water in my face and put on my clothes. I tried to be tranquil. But missing a plane does something to my nerves. I took a tranquilizer and went downstairs and met the cab.

"Are you sleepy, my dear? Why don't you go to bed for a while? Be tranquil."

Well, it seems she slept on the plane. She was quite lively and ready to see Paris. I took her to a sidewalk restaurant and got her some breakfast.

By noon she was getting sleepy and I was just waking up.

"Can you stay awake until two? We are having some pictures taken in a new Renault that is going on the market next year."

At two o'clock the photographer arrived with a new red Florida.

She was so bushed she nearly fell off the seat. I tore my pants catching her.

I went back to my room and put on some other pants and called the maid.

"Be tranquil!" she cried. "I go to mend the pants."

I took another Miltown and went to bed. I had just got to sleep when the maid came back. She said to be tranquil. The housekeeper was now examining my pants and would give a report.

I took off my pants again and went back to bed.

I had just got to sleep again when the housekeeper knocked. I put on my pants and let her in. She said all the invisible weavers of Paris were now invisible—mainly being on vacation since this was August.

She advised me to try again in September. Meanwhile, be tranquil.

I took an aspirin and went back to bed.

I had just fallen asleep again when the phone rang.

"Daddy? I'm all awake now. I had a long nap. Where are we going?"

I got up and took a bath and another tranquilizer.

We went up to Montmartre for dinner where I found the atmosphere so tranquil I fell asleep over the soup and just about embarrassed everybody to death. "Gosh," she said, "you could at least stay awake. You haven't done anything all day!"

Normandy is the eating country of France. And we have been eating elegantly: *Moules à la crème*—they take these mussels and steam them in a rich bath of cream and butter and chopped shallots.

Each morning my teen-age daughter puts on her Bermudas and lets out a horrid cry. (The times I have cut myself shaving over minor crises!)

"What is the matter?"

I sort of expect to find her hanging from a knotted noose on the chandelier. But no. She is only looking at herself in profile in the mirror.

"I can't wear Bermudas!"

"You *are* wearing Bermudas." That is logic. Logic only infuriates her.

"I *mean* I can't wear Bermudas because I am getting too *big.*"

"Stop eating." That is more logic. Anyway, I am not worried. She does not look fat to me.

"Oh, you don't understand!" That is one of the tragedies that has come to us with our teens. Used to be I had quite a rapport with this child. But now, in my dotage, I am a shell of the man I was. No understanding. Apt to positively embarrass *everybody* with those loud shirts and—oh, well.

Our problem is not only the *moules à la crème*—they come in this hot butter and cream, slightly open. You get a pair of the shells and use them like tongs to tong out the meat from the others.

Oh, yes. You save *one* empty shell, and scoop up a little of that rich soup and drink it.

What was I saying? Oh, the *moules* are not the only problem. There is the duck cooked on an open fire. It is drenched with a cream and orange sauce.

We also have a good deal of trouble with the *fraises du bois*—wild strawberries.

We are sure they are not fattening. But what do they do here but *cover* them with about two inches of cream Chantilly.

Most of the cooking in Normandy is done in cream. That is why we cannot wear Bermudas.

We dine in a Norman courtyard. Shaded by Normandy apple trees. The sea lies 100 yards away. We are living in Villerville, a few miles from the rich in Deauville.

We live at Chez Mahu. It rates a one-star restaurant with Michelin. High praise. Deauville itself has *no* one-star restaurants. They have a four crossed fork-and-spoon restaurant—for elegance. Stars are for food.

We eat the big lunch under the apple trees. Then we nap. (And that doesn't help you reduce, believe me.)

In the evening, we rise and look out the open French windows into the courtyard.

If things look lively below, we go down and join the fun. Then we eat again.

"You can't help getting fat here," she moaned.

Fat is not the problem. I have it from Denise, the pretty French girl who waits on our table.

"*C'est la foie*," she says sagely. "Watch out for the liver."

The French are greatly concerned with their livers. (Like we are with our stomachs.) Most of the bottle waters emphasize that they are better than Hadacol for the liver.

Also *les enfants*. Children, I guess, must watch their livers too.

With all this attention to livers, the French raise sand with their geese. Developing livers in them that would make a British colonel beat the natives.

They take these geese and *stuff* them with corn. This gives the goose a liver like a football. The French then stand him against the wall. Or something.

They take his liver and make *pâté de foie gras* with truffles.

It is delicious before dinner. In the Norman courtyard. And we are so full of it, we are busting out of our Bermudas.

This is packing day. At least it will be packing day when we get around to packing.

The morning Paris paper has interviewed two American college girls. They travel with 20 pounds of luggage apiece. They are organized like IBM. What jewels!

My own jewel is still sacked out. Reading a movie magazine. She worries like mad about Eddie and Liz and asks me constantly: "Will it last?" That is why we cannot get around to packing this morning. She is deep in a throbber called: "Why Liz Cried the Day After Her Wedding."

You cannot interrupt that sort of thing to stuff clothes in a bag.

The Paris journal interviewed Peggy Young and Becky Verbecker, both twenty-two of Detroit.

They are spending ten weeks in Europe with their 20-pound luggage.

We have it listed: Two sets of drip-dry nylon underwear; nighties, negligees, swim suit, sweater.

The basic outfit is three-piece in gingham-checked nylon. It starts with a scoop-neck play suit which converts to a cocktail frock when you add a matching full skirt. Also to match, a shirt blouse which makes a tailored dress with the skirt.

The other outfit is a Dacron-and-cotton shirt and a full skirt.

Each girl carried a washable raincoat in pastel colors.

Each had one evening gown.

Each had one pair of Bermudas, walking shoes, dress shoes, roll-up casuals and enough shampoo for four-times-a-week washing.

Of the 20 pounds, five were camera equipment.

My teen-age moppet is organized, too. But I cannot quite figure her weight allowance. It changes.

In Deauville, I found her buying a 10-foot fishing net on a pole.

"How will you get it home?"

"Carry it. Or put it in my suitcase."

"How will you get it in your suitcase, pray tell?"

"Well, you know. Now stop *worrying!* I'm grown-up and can take care of things."

One of the best ways we take care of things is by saying: "Here, hold this for a minute."

That works just fine. Only then your father gets mad and is horrid.

"How many dresses did you bring?" I am interviewing through the connecting doorway.

"Why?" (There's a female answer for you.)

"I will ask the questions. How many?"

"About five or seven. Or eight."

"HOW MANY!"

"Do you want me to get up and count them?"

"I want a square answer. I warn you—"

"I think it is six. Listen, do you think they were *really* in love. Or was it infatugation?"

"Who? What is infatugation?"

"Eddie and Liz. Were they victims of infatugation—like just swept off their feet but not true love?"

"How the— I mean, concentrate. What else do you carry?"

Well, it seems we carry shoes. About three or six pairs, we can't remember. Omigosh! That reminds us. We have some shoes being mended up at that place—where is it? "Will you go get them for me? Please!"

"Get them yourself." I am cold and cruel.

"But I'm not *dressed.*"

"Get dressed. Put on one of those five or seven or nine or whatever dresses. Look at the paper. Look at these organized Detroit girls. *They* know what they will wear. And I'll bet they get up and pack in the morning."

"Gosh, you're mean. I guess it is probably just infatugation. Isn't that sad?"

You can say that again.

"Do I have to go back to school?"

That is the voice of my teen-age girl child from the next room. The voice of despair. The fall of leaves reminds her of the stern call of education. Oh, dear.

We distributed a few silver dollars among the helpful hotel help. You should carry a few silver dollars—they are the ginchiest. The most.

I distribute them to the maid, the room waiter, the room

waiter's assistant, and the man who shows up out of nowhere just as I start to leave. It seems he has been shining the shoes we leave outside the door in the hall.

A sort of message goes through the hotel when I pick up the first pair of socks to put in the suitcase. A bamboo telegraph.

"The man with the silver dollars is checking out."

How did they know I was checking out? I swear all I did was pick up one little old pair of socks. And the room filled up like a convention.

The little emergency empty space in my flight bag is a godsend to female relatives.

I am organized. Executive. I look forward.

I leave a little bit of room in my flight bag.

Isn't that wonderful? Because it seems that our daughter suddenly found something she forgot to pack. And the bags have already gone downstairs.

It is one of those flouncy petticoats.

"Don't smash it! Don't crush it!"

Did you ever try to get one of these things into half a flight bag? It calls for the delicacy of a diamond cutter.

"Do you have your ticket, my dear? How about your passport? Keep it handy."

Well, would you believe it? It seems we packed the ticket and the passport.

"You *said* to keep it safe. So I packed it because that was the safest place. Gosh! You don't have to practically *scream* like that!"

We were heading for the elevator when the maid came running after us.

She had a white bobby sock in her hand. It was wet, too. A relic from the drying rack in the bathroom.

Our child was mortified. She mortifies easily. And to be handed a wet sock in an elevator full of people!

Anyway, we drove out to Orly through the warm, lighted boulevards where the leaves drifted silently in the night.

(It only took a *minute* to unpack the bags and get the passport and tickets. Only then we couldn't get it all back in again. But our father had some room in his flight bag only you would think it was *gold* or something. The way he talked.)

And we got on the big TWA plane with the engines giving that big surge of power as you go down the runway.

And so up into the night. With the lights of France below. Then Ireland and the runways of Shannon. And all across the northern sky there was a thin band of daylight.

Until morning when we came down through the sparkling sunlight into New York.

You know the first thing we did? Headed for Hamburger Heaven and had a *big* hamburger. With everything on it.

8.

WE live in an age of instant marvels. Coffee by the instant. Soup by the second. Stir, pour and let sit a half hour in the refrigerator.

Nobody has come up with an answer for man's most pressing need: Instant money.

The quickest way to get instant cash is to fish around under the cushions in an upholstered chair. I seldom come up with less than a dime—once we hit for two half dollars!

Under car seats sometimes produce a little ready. But for the sheer joy of skin diving and discovery, there is nothing like an overstuffed couch.

In London some time back, the repairman went over to Buckingham Palace. The Palace is that enormous scatter where tourists go to watch the Guards change.

Anyway, you can figure with a place that size, there is always some kind of repair going on. The plumbing alone— well, no use going into all those problems.

The job this time was to repair a sofa.

They took off the covers. Inside, in the stuffing, was a note:

This sofa was last repaired in the reign of William IV.

William was King from 1830 to 1837.

First thing that occurred to me was, "How much did they find down along the sides?" You know the part you stick your hand in and *Ouch!* You get stuck with a pin.

No mention was made of more than the note. But it stands to reason a sofa that has been collecting since 1830–37 must have been a treasure trove.

Another thing that occurs to an ordinary householder: How come that sofa has not been touched for 130 years?

In our neighborhood, we re-cover chairs and couches almost constantly.

We put on new covers because we are tired of the old ones.

We put on new covers because there is a sale on covering material. And, if you look at it right, it really *saves* money to cover now.

We cover because:

"For heaven's sake, we just put on new covers a week ago!"

"It was six *months* ago. Anyway, the Scofflaws just *bought* a whole new living room set!"

Re-cover or die of shame.

In choosing a chair or sofa, we recommend the deep stuffed lean-back type.

The back should be made of soft stuffing—so that the user's pockets will empty easily. The seat cushions should be of firmer material. If the user sinks deeply, the change will gather under him.

The idea is to maintain comfort and, at the same time, a

gradual slope of the cushion toward the back edge. The money should not lie there. It should disappear.

A proper chair or sofa is better than a savings bank.

Of next importance is the user. Women should not be allowed to sit in the chair—though they may use one spot on the three-cushion sofa. They must sit in the middle. Put the men on the side so that loose change has a chance to roll either backwards or sidewards.

Put a lighter or ash tray just out of reach.

When the lady needs a cigarette, both gentlemen lean forward for the item.

This gentle back and forward movement massages the pockets and empties them.

With attention to these little details, a substantial nest egg can be built up under the cushions. It will be a great help in the re-covering.

"What are some good points about my character?" This question is flung at me from an upstairs window where my teen-age daughter is doing her homework.

We do our homework to 45-speed records. "He's got tan shoes with pink shoelaces . . . hat with a purple band."

"I have to write a composition about my character."

"Why don't you write when I am good I am a doll? And when I am bad I am a slob?"

Well, it seems we have written down all the bad things. Like: "Sometimes I am lazy. Or sometimes I get mad at people for nothing—you don't have to nod your head like that, Father—and now I need the good things."

You know, we thought and we thought. We could not think of all the good things.

"Would you say, 'I am capable of lofty sentiments and strong infections?'"

"That is an excellent characteristic," I said. "Why didn't we think of that?"

"I read it in a book," she said, sadly. "I don't suppose it is really like me.

"Would you say I was a good counselor in times of distress?"

"I would, indeed. Your counsel has pulled me over many a reef of distress. Put that down before you forget it."

"Would you say I was kind and obedient?"

"Well—"

"All right. I'll take that out."

Heavenly days, I am glad I do not have to write a composition called "My Character."

"How many words does it have to be?" I yelled at the window.

". . . wears a polka dot vest and pink shoelaces," answered the phonograph.

"What?"

"HOW MANY WORDS?"

"I don't know. It has to be two pages."

"You have two propositions: If you are getting paid by the word—as for magazines—then you should run it back and forth. Like, you say, 'I have lofty sentiments and strong infections. But, on the other hand—' Then you knock it down.

"If you are getting paid by the piece, write it in big longhand and don't say much. But take up a lot of space."

"That would not be fair," she said.

"That is my character," I said simply.

After a while I went up out of the sun and read the manuscript:

> Many people think they know what makes John, Mary and Dick tick. But they don't know much about themselves. In this composition I will tell you about my character.

That is a straightforward lead. I particularly like the "Dick tick" part. It is kind of poetic.

The composition went on to list various faults. I tell you it was about all a strong man could stand.

How about all the good things? Like you are kind to me and to animals?

It seems being kind to your father and animals is not character. Character is something people have in movies. Like when the girl says, "Go. Your duty lies with the girl you left in Malaya."

Unfortunately, nothing like that has ever happened to us. So we have little character.

At the end of the piece, she wrote:

> I am very sympathic. I don't believe anybody can tell what their character really is.

Neither do I. I am very sympathic on that point.

"The problem is," said the lady with a frown, "you do not have that much money in your account."

"That is a mighty weak excuse," I said. "Here we have a relationship between the World's Largest Bank and the World's Smallest Customer. And you talk about lack of money."

The lady looked worried.

"It is against the rules to give you money unless you have some money here."

That is the problem with banks—always worried about how the books will turn out at the end of the day.

"Have you looked in the mail?" I asked. "I mailed a check in yesterday. Maybe it slipped down behind a file cabinet. Or in the wastebasket."

It was not as though I wanted to ease them out of some money. I really had mailed a deposit check. And now I wanted to take it out. That is a businesslike attitude.

I wanted to take it out and buy travelers' checks. Right from the same bank.

"I will only use it for a little while. Just to walk to the next window and give it to the man who will take it right back into your bank. And then give me travelers' checks."

I said she could come with me so I could not cheat. She could come with me and hold my hand. She could even bring the private policeman along. I would even let them handcuff me.

No. She was worried because the books did not show I had the same amount of money I had on my check.

People walk into banks all over our town and hand in a folded note:

> You are covered from all sides! Fill the sack with large bills!

These are criminal people—a little daffy. Few professional heisters go around heisting banks because it is a very bad rap and the FBI makes life miserable until they collar you.

I mean if I were going to be criminal about this affair, I would have handed the lady a note:

Have gun. Will travel. Where do I get the travelers' checks?

No, sir. I went in square as Jack the bear.

"If I go back to my office and get another check and deposit it, will you let me draw some money then?"

The lady said yes. She would do that, certainly.

And that is what I did. Went back and wrote a check for deposit. Went back and deposited it. Then I gave her the check for withdrawal. Got the money. Walked down and gave it back to the bank.

And they gave me some travelers' checks. It takes a certain amount of brains.

The world's first and only incorporated dog arrived at our house yesterday afternoon. He is two months old, black-and-white and described vaguely as:

"He is Australian shepherd. Only partly he is something else."

I am advised by my heiress to love and cherish this dog.

To forget that one side of his family may not have registered in the Social Register.

To love him for himself alone. "And be sure to keep water in his dish."

With this parting advice, she took off for school. The pup lay down and began to chew the telephone cord in two.

For quite a while now, we have discussed a dog for my son. Like all household projects, it caused more clucking than a hen house at egg-laying time.

Nobody could agree on what *kind* of dog.

We had advocates of toy poodles that matched the car

upholstery. We had the great Dane set. Neighbors got in the act and offered Airedales, Chihuahuas and English bulldogs.

I tell you everybody was on edge. Ready to *scream* if you mentioned dog again.

Well, this was all solved by the Miss Fixit of the scatter. She simply came in from the country the other day carrying this "Australian shepherd only partly something else."

There were some halfhearted tries to return the dog but the female child burst into tears. The small boy, seeing this, roared off into sobs himself.

And before you could gather your wits, the pup was drinking milk, had a seat by the fire and was giving a fair imitation of an orphan out of the storm.

There was also some talk about who would pay the board-and-room on a dog. A dog can cut a chunk out of a household budget that can hardly hook up the back anyway.

"Daddy will pay for it out of the corporation," said my daughter.

The corporation is an elastic catchall. We couldn't get along without it.

At some grandiose moment, I got a corporation. It has never made a dime. But, like a dog, it is a handy thing to have around the house.

For some reason, there is an unshakable opinion around here that a corporation is like an unlimited bank account.

"The corporation only has $10 in the whole bank account!" I cried.

Well, that is silly. *Everybody* knows a corporation is a rich old thing. Owned by rich people. And papers are always writing: CORPORATE EARNINGS REACH ALL TIME HIGH.

I am suspected of holding out vast riches in this incorporated mystery.

The dog has been named Inc., a likely monicker for an incorporated dog.

He does not match the seat covers. He could not get into the American Kennel Club even if a member vouched for him and offered to sign for the lunch.

Being a pup, you cannot tell yet how big he will grow or what shape he will come out. But—

"We got him for free! And the corporation can pay for his food."

I think I will turn over the corporation secretly to Inc. He can be president. He can be chairman of the board.

At present he does not wish to be either. He wishes to chew telephone cords. Likely that dog has a piece of A. T. & T.

The Sunday Afternoon Musical Appreciation Society met in our living room Saturday night. They brought their sleeping bags.

The Sunday Afternoon Musical Appreciation Society is made up of young ladies who appreciate good music. Particularly those little 45-speed records with the big hole in the center.

> . . . *treat me like an overgrown child,*
> . . . *my kissing drives you wild.*

That is the music we appreciate most.

The Society gets into their sleeping bags and turns up the phonograph full volume. Sigh! Sigh! Sigh!

"Isn't it just DEEEEEEvine!"

The Society is made up of the same members who used to be members of the Redwood Terrace Club. This was an organization when these same ladies were younger.

The former club was devoted to selling Kool-Aid (mostly to me). Also rescuing lost cats, discussing boys, and other good works.

I am now an honorary member and financial secretary of the Musical Appreciation Society.

We started out some years ago with a demand that I buy nails and lumber for Custer's Last Stand and Lone Ranger Club.

As we grew older, we went into the lemonade business. It turned out badly. As financial advisor and well-wisher to the Redwood Terrace Club, I became almost 100 per cent pure lemon juice.

Well, now we are all older. And we look back with kindly laughter on those days when we were young.

Two things have not changed over the years: The members still talk about boys; I am still the financial genius. *Somebody* has to pay for the records.

The records, by the way, are rock 'n' roll.

This is a curious music of our times. All of it sung in a panting monotone by teen-age boys who make a whopping fortune.

> *Umpa-umpa, still go to school*
> *Umpa-umpa I'm no fool. . . .*

That is the way the records sound to me. That is why I am only an honorary member. No appreciation.

Anyway, we had nine members of the Society in sleeping bags the other night. The lights turned low and the volume turned up. They kept a little record for me: Poor. Fair. Great. Divine!

Under Divine! I find a Mr. Johnnie Strickland singing "You've Got What It Takes." My correspondents add that it is "slow yet fast feeling.")

"That's Love" is also divine. It is sung by Paul Anka. When I said, "Who is Paul Anka?" I nearly got read out of the Society.

We also gave a divine rating to something called "The Great Healer." And to a Mr. Buddy Knox singing "That's Why I Cry."

I could not understand from the umpa-umpa lyrics just why he was crying. But I came close to weeping, myself. About the time they put the record on for the sixteenth time. The Society adjourned the meeting at midnight. It was unanimously voted to thank the host and financial secretary for getting the records. He was also advised to bring a lot of new cool records to the next meeting.

The Appreciation Society then turned out the lights and turned off the phonograph. The financial secretary appreciated that. More than he can tell.

I think it was one of those *How to Raise Your Child* books where I read:

"Everything your child does has a motive."

At dawn this morning, the boy rose quietly and squeezed a full tube of green ointment into his hair. It is a peculiar chemical that will not wash out. His head looks like a growing lawn.

I have looked into his motives but can find no dark spots on his psyche.

The way I figure his motives is like this: When you get a tube and there are no grownups around, *squeeze it!*

He put it in his hair as an afterthought. I am glad he did not eat it.

If you have a well-cared-for ax and a few ladies around the house, that ax will show up eventually, dull and rusty as an after-dinner speech.

Not only that. Every female within sight will screech that *she* never touches that ax. It is a male instrument. Never used by ladies.

Why, then, is the blade chipped? And why does the head fly off the handle? One of life's mysteries, gentlemen.

I have noticed that tools disappear in this order: First the hammer is gone. Next the screw driver evaporates.

One day you hear a banging in the living room. You peek through the window. The lady is hanging pictures. With the ax.

"I can't find the hammer," she says logically. Bang! Bang!

The hammer is on the top shelf of the closet. The ladies used it one day to fix a shoe heel. The screw driver is on a canned-goods shelf. It seems one day the can opener was lost and we tried to open the can with . . .

You asked me how the ax blade got chipped? Well, the dresser drawer stuck and we pried it open.

The ax was then slung out under a wet tree to rust.

Everybody denies this.

I have spent a good deal of my life with zippers and buttons. For reasons known only to heaven, ladies' dresses are fastened where she cannot possibly reach. In the back.

If it were not for fathers, young ladies would never get married.

I spent my youth buttoning my mother up the back.

Have now come full circle and am zipping my daughter up the back.

Young men do not know about this zipper proposition. Nor that they will be expected to take over some day. They live in a fool's paradise—the package is delivered for the dance already gift-wrapped.

The zipping is easy enough. But at the top is a tiny, tiny hook. Does this hook slip into a metal eye? Ha! It hooks onto a tiny loop of dark thread. So small you can hardly see it with a magnifying glass.

While you are hooking, the wearer is wiggling into makeup.

"Hold still! I can't find it."

"It's right there!"

What a life!

What I cannot understand is how the manufacturers make such flimsy catches.

A dress that costs the price of a small piece of real estate is hooked by a thread. For the price it should have golden gaskets.

Milady is now dressed. Zipped and hooked.

She walks down the stairs packing a small suitcase called a handbag. It is the latest model. It cost a fortune.

Without touching this valise, mind you—without laying a pinkie on it—the thing suddenly opens. It opens in a curious way. It falls apart. It dumps the contents like a dump truck unloading cement.

"Oh! How did that happen?"

It happens ten times a day. But the lady is covered with delicate confusion. So delicate she can only stand there while everybody goes under the couch for the lipstick.

Yet she can hang pictures with an ax. Isn't that amazing?

"I am in desperate trouble and I don't know who to turn to," she said on the telephone.

Well, that is my desperate child, all right. She has been in desperate straits as long as I can remember.

"I don't know who to turn to," she said desperately.

"Don't turn to me," I cried. "Turn to the President. Or Uncle Walter Ramage, who is a pigeon for your woes. The last time you turned to me, it got me in trouble."

"Daddy!" she said. The knife in the back.

"Oh, well," I said weakly. "What is it?"

Having gained this advantage, you could hear her voice settle down. She was winners and she knew it.

"Well, you know Mother's Bermuda shorts? The new linen ones?"

"Go on."

"Well, it wasn't my fault. Honest. It was the waitress."

"What waitress?"

"The waitress in the restaurant. She spoke to me and I turned around."

"What about the Bermudas?"

"That's what I'm trying to *tell* you, if you'll just listen. You see, I didn't have *anything* to wear. And we wanted to go to this restaurant, you know? Just for a little snack in the afternoon.

"I thought you were on a diet."

"I am. But—well, anyway. Will you listen? I'm in desperate trouble and I don't know *who* to turn to."

"You have already turned, my dear," I said. "So turn off the tears and the soap opera. Your loving father has saddled up the horses. The cavalry is about to ride over the horizon."

"Anyway, it *wasn't* my fault," she said. "Only the fork slipped just a little."

"Is this a history of your life?" I said politely.

"I'm trying to *tell* you."

"Tell then."

"We went down to this restaurant. And I don't know what happened. But the waitress spoke to me and I looked around. Or maybe she pushed me. Just accidentally a little.

"Anyway," she said desperately, "the blueberry pie went on the shorts."

"On your mother's new Bermudas?"

"Yes, Daddy."

"You borrowed them?"

"Yes, Daddy."

"And you didn't ask first?"

"No, Daddy. But I *couldn't*. Because she was out. And I didnt have a *thing* to wear and—"

"Boy! Are *you* going to catch it!" I said cheerfully.

"Oh, Daddy!"

Well, that is the way it goes. Out of Mr. Bell's magic instrument comes the voice of doom: "I am in desperate trouble."

Was a time when the child's confiding woes filled me with alarm. But I have become hardened over the years. A man could not stand the emotion I am called upon to handle.

The time the cat caught the pet lizard and wouldn't give it back. The time the guppy went down the bathtub drain.

(We kept these fish in the bathtub and it gave you a peculiar feeling when you took a bath.)

There was the time we tore the party dress. And the time we put salt instead of sugar in the Kool-Aid at the Kool-Aid stand.

I advised her to call the cleaner and ask for advice.

The cleaner is a younger, cleaner man. I've got to have assistance in this business. My emotions are all ground down. I am desperate and don't know who to turn to.

I have not received a report card in quite a time. I do hope everything is going well in the educational field where I planted the flower of my flock.

"They expect you to learn *everything!* How can a person possibly learn *everything?*"

That is the anguished cry from aloft. The voice of our dreams of posterity.

It is homework time.

The house is hushed—except for the gentle splish-splosh, splish-splosh of the washing machine. Temperament spills down the stairs in a flood you can almost feel.

"Oh! I give up!" *Slam!* That is the door. (But I can tighten the hinges again tomorrow.)

Used to be I helped on the homework. That was when it was simple stuff.

Like: "Bob lost three-fifths of his money and had $3 left. How much had he at first?"

Well, it is laughable. But I never could work that one out. And after a while I gave it up.

Anyway, I do not think schools should send children home to annoy their fathers with such material. Also, I do not think children should study about people who lose three-fifths of their money.

How did he lose it? Off-track betting?

Why do we study about people who bet the bangtails when they have only three skins left when they are through? People like that should not bet at all.

If he did not lose it to the bookie, how did he manage to lose exactly three-fifths? Answer me that. He lost three-fifths with the books. And he saved $3 so he could take a taxi home. A spendthrift.

I hardly dare peek into the schoolbooks these days, I am that ignorant.

I have a vague feeling I went through these things once. But am happy to report I have forgotten all of it.

The things I went through learning about "a" square plus "b" square . . . !

In all my mature years, *nobody* has asked me the square root of anything.

Nobody laughs when I sit down at the slide rule. And I have never been humilated with questions of just what Cornwallis said to Washington. (I think he said, "George, you ought to try *my* dentist.")

I forget which side the hypotenuse is buttered on.

But I am high on morals and I attribute this to a thorough study of Horatio G. Alger. That is what counts in the long run—principles.

There do not seem to be any books of this caliber for girls and boys these televised days. But when I was searching for truth, we counted on Horatio.

The boy heroes of the Alger books were "Poor But Honest"—I think that was a title. They sold papers to support their widowed mothers and shivered pathetically in the winter winds.

"A newspaper, sir?"

"Why yes, my lad. Here is a penny, my good fellow. Is it not late for you to be abroad with only a thin sweater? I fear you shall take a cold."

"Oh, no, sir," said the brave lad. "You see I *must* sell these papers. For my dear mother is waiting to pay the rent."

That is the kind of dialogue I was educated on. And when I joined the journalism field, I found it went just as well as ever.

You may remember that Horatio's shivering boy found that the elderly gentleman had slipped him a $3 gold piece instead of a penny. He followed him through snow and ice to return the golden coin. And was rewarded by being made vice-president in charge of $3 gold pieces.

With this education, I got into journalism first by selling papers myself. And once a man gave me a dime instead of a penny. But by running very slow, I managed to avoid returning it because he got on a streetcar.

I could see that my fortune was made. I had been on the right educational track all along.

9.

WE have been caught up in the social whirl these holi-
days, your social correspondent whirling with a great deal of
grace, if I do say so myself.

It seems we have invited six boys and five girls to dinner
—my own teen-age daughter filling out the extra place.

Such advance preparations! You would think I had never
been to parties.

"What will you wear?" she asked anxiously.

"Why, my dear, I think I will wear something attractive
but informal. Like my old bathrobe."

"Daddy!"

"I will also tell sprightly jokes. If pressed, I will play the
guitar. I will play 'If He Can Fight Like He Can Love, Look
Out Germany!'"

Well, it seems this is not the idea at all. I am only to look
presentable.

Wait for my entrance music. Get on stage and get off.
Quietly.

I can report that the party went off well. The young ladies
arrived starched and ruffled. The young gentlemen were
shined and pressed.

The young ladies had been dressing for hours and hours.
But they took one look at this array of talent and galloped
upstairs to repair imaginary details.

The gentlemen and I stood around downstairs and made
small talk.

"Where do you go to school?"

"Drake."

"Oh."

Nobody asked me where I go to school. I go to the School
of Hard Knocks and Ungrateful Children. But nobody
asked me.

Nobody asked me to play the guitar. They put on a record
instead.

She's got buck teeth. She's cross-eyed.
Look out, gang. Here she comes.

To my mind, this cannot compare with "Lucky Lindy."
Which I would have been glad to play at the drop of a guitar
string.

Over the ocean he flew like a cloud,
That sort of boy makes a mother feel proud . . .

The young ladies returned and I joined them to make so-
ciable conversation.

"Well, well," I said heartily, "I am not used to seeing all
you girls with all your clothes on."

"Father!"

"What I mean," I said hastily, "is you are usually around here in jeans or shorts. Not dressed up."

My daughter gave me a warning look. I excused myself and went out to the kitchen and poured myself a small glass of the cooking sherry.

Why, I remember these girls when they sold lemonade out in our road. I remember one of them falling down the hill and breaking her arm. I remember. But I am not allowed to talk about it.

In fact, there are a number of things I am not allowed to even remember. Let alone print.

I am not allowed to reminisce about some of my fascinating adventures. Or what happened when I went to school. Or play the guitar.

I am not even allowed to dance. I am just supposed to sit around in the ashes. Like Cinderella. While everybody else goes to the ball.

The ladies then excused themselves. They disappeared upstairs and made extensive changes in make-up and costume.

They came down and announced they were now ready to attend the dance.

Guess who was permitted to drive them. In a big, four-door pumpkin with white sidewalls.

And so, back to the ashes.

Having given way to a perfect frenzy of Christmas shopping lately, I have decided to make this a day of rest.

On such a day, you get up and make the coffee. You get the papers. Pour the coffee. Get back into bed. Such luxury.

In Halifax, England, neighbors discovered Mr. Matthew Sutcliffe sacked up and happy in the old homestead.

"Why, Matt," they said, "didn't you used to be a railroad porter wot we 'ave not seen in 30 blinkin' years, God wot?" they said.

"Aye," said Matthew. For it was indeed he.

He said he caught a cold 30 years ago and went to bed. He liked it so well he just never got up.

He spent all his time reading the papers and following the football pools.

Matthew had the right idea.

The day you decide to stay in bed is the day the plumber cometh. He cometh with a long length of wire and a suction pump.

"Use your phone?" he said.

"Help yourself."

The plumber sat on the bed and dialed his number.

"You sick?" he said. "Hey, Charlie? Charlie, looks like a root stoppage. Yep. We may have to tear up the flooring. Yep. Yep. You sick?" he said to me.

"I am resting."

"You look sick," said the plumber critically. "Just like my wife's brother. Just felt off his feed, he said. Stayed in bed for a couple of days. By the time we called the doctor it was too late."

"What was wrong with him?" I said weakly.

"Twisted something inside himself," said the plumber.

"I feel excellent. I just want a day off."

"Looks like the roots from the oak tree punched through into the drain," said the plumber. "I always say in the morning, 'If you can get up, get up.' Who knows when the day comes you can't lift a pinkie from the covers.

"That drain is gonna cost you," said the plumber, lighting a cigarette and settling down on the edge of the bed. "You should never put in terra-cotta drains. Roots punch through them like paper."

"It is a little late to take up the house and put in new drains now."

"You may have to eventually," said the plumber cheerfully. "Seen it time and again. Water backed up all over the place and the kids coming down with pneumonia. This brother-in-law of mine, you'd think he was living forever. Husky sorta fella. Never sick a day in his life.

"Went to bed one day for a rest—like you. 'I'll just take a short rest,' he said. Two days later—Hark, he heard the angels sing.

"He had his insurance paid up though."

"My insurance is paid up," I said. "When do you think you can open that drain?"

"Gotta wait for the equipment. Keep the insurance paid up, that's my motto. You can't take it with you. But it gives you a good feeling. You always flushed like that?"

"What flush?" I said, getting up and looking in the mirror. The plumber took one of my pillows and put it behind his head. He lit another of my cigarettes.

"Sorta red-faced. Like high blood pressure. Pressure is the one that knocks them off."

"I feel great," I said dizzily. "Shouldn't you look at the drain?"

"If you don't mind," said the plumber, "I'll just sit here on the bed and read the papers till my partner gets here with the equipment. I been working myself to a frazzle," said the plumber, "and I can use the rest."

I got up and put on my clothes and went down to look at

the drain. If you ask me, that plumber should watch himself. He didn't look good, lying back there on my bed. You know what I mean? Things can hit you when you least expect them. Pop! Just like that.

While my aching back was turned, while I was out toiling and slaving, a Christmas tree was purchased and brought into the house.

It has been pointed out to me for hours by trained decorators that this tree *does* something for the house. Its price has been held up as part of its quality. I have been asked do I want to be a Scrooge? Do I want to *spoil* everybody's Christmas?

I am unyielding.

"What's *wrong* with the tree?"

"It's not *green*, blast it!"

How can you call a tree a Christmas tree when it is not green? When it is metallic bronze? Or pink? Or silver?

I tell you, household ladies go wild about such trees.

They can picture this metal monster gleaming in the living room (and blending just right with the andirons and that light we have in the corner, don't you see?)— the fact that all the globes are one color intrigues them, too.

"Just this big splash of bronze with golden balls!"

We came mighty close to having a pink tree with silver-ice globes. But we decided against it because it would clash with the dress we intend to wear Christmas Eve.

That is the way Christmas trees are chosen these days. When this cat's away at work. And all the mice get a surge of decorative instinct by reading a lot of lame-brain articles in the women's magazines:

"Make Your Tree a Pageant of Christmas!"

What has happened to the soft green Christmas tree we loved so well? The tree we hung with many-colored lights and many-colored balls?

The tree you sprayed with silver where you wanted it. A splash here, a splash there. A splash on the dog and a little on the child. Merry Christmas, dog! Merry Christmas, child!

Gone but not forgotten. Fare thee well.

"What, pray tell, will we do with the old ornaments?" I said with the voice I am able to serve a good deal below room temperature.

Well, it is the strangest thing. It seems that all the old ornaments were *old*, see? They were outmoded. And most of them were broken, anyway.

And besides, I am the only one who is against a metallic tree. If I would just *try* and let it grow on me . . . It was just to make Christmas different for *me*. Sniff. Sniff.

I am a hard man. Steel spring. I am not impressed with colored Christmas trees.

I do not give a hoot that all the neighbor ladies have been around, ooh-ing and ah-ing. (And jealous as all get out—heh, heh, I will bet they put the bite on their breadwinners for a solid gold tree. Gad, what trouble there will be in the neighborhood!)

I do not care if these ladies do think this tree is gorgeous.

I do not care if this tree blends with the wallpaper.

It does not blend with my spirit. It does not blend with my everygreen personality.

Bring me back my green Christmas tree!

I want a tree I can climb on a shaky ladder and put a big silver star on top. A tree you have to *work* with to cover the bare spots—you know, put a red ball over here and a blue

214

one there and move that string of lights up on the next branch.

I do not want pink trees, silver trees, gold trees or bronze trees.

I do not want predecorated trees with balls all one golden glitter.

You ever hear about Midas? Was he happy? Well!

Somebody robbed the piggy bank. For Christmas, my male moppet got a handsome brass bank with a padlock on it. There was a silver dollar inside—you could rattle it around and it made a noble sound.

We kept the key tied to the bank. You know how easy it is to lose keys. And this seemed the best way to keep it.

Anyway, I shook the bank the other day. (I wanted to hear the dollar rattle, that's all; so don't look at *me*.)

It did not rattle. The key was there and the padlock wide open.

Well, nobody knows how to handle these things better than me. I had just gone to a movie called *A Touch of Larceny*. I knew just how a British fuzz acts.

"We must ahsk you nawt to leave the premises." You know. That kind of underplay.

Everybody denied the crime. In fact, they all got indignant.

"Who, me? I did *not!*"

"That dollar didn't walk away," I said. "Now look: If you *borrowed* it, it is okay. But I want it back."

I tell you, there were protests and weeping. But I put a hot, white light in their faces and said I would send them up for 20 years if they wanted it the hard way.

It is still a mystery. Our son denies it. But other times he says maybe he opened the bank. And sometimes he says he thinks the neighbor's cat took it. A cool customer, that child.

The New York press agents who flacked the picture *A Touch of Larceny* had a good idea.

They got ten wallets. They stuffed each wallet with five $1 bills. They put in a card with a return address and phone number. Then they dropped these wallets on the sidewalks of New York.

They also hid around the corner and watched the finders.

Seven people picked up the wallets and telephoned.

Two men and one woman grabbed the planted pokes and disappeared.

That is a good game. I wish I had thought of it.

When I was a moppet, we used to stuff a snap purse with newspaper. We put it on the sidewalk and tied a heavy thread to it. Then we hid around the corner with the thread in our hand.

When somebody bent over for the purse, we snatched it away with the thread.

One thing I recall well: *Before* each person leaned down to get that purse, they took a long look around to see if anybody was looking.

Well, I am not casting any first stones. Tripping down memory lane, it seems to me I used to heist my mother's purse once in a while.

It is not the money or the morals, entirely. My reputation as a sleuth is at stake. ("Scotland Yard depends on you, my boy," said the Inspector. "Dash it all, we *must* find those diamonds!")

I questioned our teen-age daughter. She needed a dollar.

She has important needs. Like lipstick and shows and things like that.

She got so mad she would not speak to me.

The boy is the prime suspect. Of course, it is his dollar. And he can open anything. He can open a can of sardines *without* the key.

"Let's play a game, son. *How* did you get the bank to open?"

This time he said he did not do it. Never touched the bank. He has a childish, innocent look. A small angel. He did not do it. But he knows who did.

"Who was it, son? I will never tell that you ratted on your accomplice."

He says it was the milkman.

Just to show you it's the same the whole world over, friends send me a clip from the Melbourne, Australia, papers:

The average sixteen-year-old schoolgirl spends about two hours and a half on the telephone each week.

The Melbourne paper is not against this—just amazed. "What do they find to talk about?" asks the editor.

That is a question, sir, which troubles me. I do not know what they talk about in Australia. But from the size of my phone bill, I suspect up here they recite the complete history of Grant's campaign around Richmond.

The Melbourne people got this information by surveying what a schoolgirl does with her leisure.

Melbourne is a leisurely town. From the air, it looks a little like England. Brick houses set in neat rows on the clean streets.

The longest oyster bar in the world is located on Flanders Street. (I know this for a fact. Because I ran up and down it, trying to break the oyster-eating record of 40 dozen per hour.)

It produces the best beer in Australia—a claim bitterly disputed by Sydney.

The main thoroughfare is Collins Street. Referred to lyrically as "tree-lined Collins Street" by Ken Macker, the American poet-publicist for the Victoria Promotion Committee.

This does not take two hours and a half to tell or talk about.

The girls must be talking about something else.

I am not allowed to listen to my own daughter's conversations. Not any more.

These telephone communications take place in another room.

There is an extension upstairs. But about every two minutes she puts her head out the door and asks suspiciously:

"Is somebody on the other phone?"

Reassured, she goes back again and I catch a fragment before the door is quite closed.

"He *did?* No, I did not! Really!"

"What were you talking about, my dear?"

"Homework."

I think Melbourne fathers are getting off easy with only two and a half hours per week.

Our telephone leisure time occupies about two and a half hours per conversation. That is the way it seems, anyway, when I am trying to get the phone.

The phone company has something called "the unit system." A most complicated arrangement of time-on-telephone times distance of call. It is impossible to figure out and would have stumped Alexander Graham Bell.

The only way you figure it out is when the bill comes in. "*What!* Ye gods, $35.60?*"

We then go into a terrific argument about why phone bills are so high. It seems *she* was only on the phone five minutes. It was a matter of life and death at that. So it must have been *my* calls.

In a clever moment, I figured a way to limit those calls. I bought an egg timer. One of those sandglass things you turn upside down. When the sand runs out, it is three minutes. She should hang up at the end of that time.

It fell down in the chair and she sat on it. Pop!

It is impossible to buy new egg timers *and* pay the phone bills, too.

It is a sort of miserable satisfaction to know this telephone ailment is not confined to my own offspring. That it is international.

That when it is winter here, it is summer in Melbourne. That we both drive on the wrong side of the street. But when it comes to our daughter's leisure time, it's Papa that pays and pays. Feel better now?

Down to the store this morning to buy Valentines. The Valentine material these wonderful days comes prearranged and packaged.

We bought package of gluey hearts and a sticky bear. He holds a heart in his paws. A balloon of words comes out of his mouth: "The bear fact is . . ."

We have an instruction book. You paste the bear on the outside of the blank Valentine card. Then on the inside you paste some more hearts and a stickered message:

I hope this finds you feeling fine
And you will be MY Valentine.

It is a nice, sentimental thought—all our thoughts seem to be prepackaged by the manufacturer these days. That is something to think about.

The Valentines are for my boy. Let it never be said that I did not give this boy a push in the right direction.

I was a fair hand at Love's windmill business myself. When I was sticking up Valentines.

I must say we did not have the equipment that is furnished to young lovers these loving days.

We worked mainly with paper doilies, red paper and flour-and-water paste.

We sent the products to the teacher and to our mothers. We made up comic ones and sent them to each other.

Roses are red, violets are blue,
Johnny Dunn is a rat and so are you.

It was hilarious stuff and we couldn't have gone through school without it.

Sometimes a girl in the class would send us a Valentine. Women are absolutely shameless.

The Valentines were turned in to the teacher. And they were passed out by the teacher. The teacher, being a woman, saw nothing wrong with calling your name and saying— the disgrace of it!—saying right before everybody:

"Here's one for you from Susie McDonnell."

You then dragged yourself from your seat. Other boys whistled and pretended to faint in the aisles. You went up and got the thing. And stumbled back to your seat.

All the way back, other boys put out their feet and tried to trip you.

At the end of the day, the biggest boy in the class would take you out behind the school and beat you up. It was considered a just punishment. I do not remember ever complaining about it.

I suppose all this must come to my own son. But in the meantime, I intend to teach him how to stick up Valentines. (That and a few handy judo holds.)

We used the lacy paper doilies for the base of our Valentines.

Then we cut red hearts out of the red paper and stuck them on with flour-and-water paste. The hearts were a little out of shape but our hearts were in it.

We really preferred the comic Valentines. My son is more concerned with the comical side of the bear holding a heart than with the sentiment.

I guess that is the masculine outlook on this loving day. And one we must keep in check.

I remember my grandfather came home with a box of candy. And with it a comic card which he thought was uproarious. It was something about a Salvation Army lass on Valentine's Day. And this man staggered out of a saloon and laid a hand on her arm. It wound up:

> *But she only said, "God bless you, sir"*
> *And placed a mark upon his brow*
> *With a kick she had learned before she was Saved.*

Grandma wouldn't speak to him for a long time.

I have our census form all filled in long before the census taker comes around.

In one out of every four homes, extra questions will be asked. That home is picked by chance, so that no one knows in advance whether it will be yours or your neighbors . . .

That is what it says on the outside of my census form.

I hope it is my home that is chosen for the extra questions. Let them ask me. I will tell them a thing or two. If they choose my neighbor, let them ask me anyway.

I know a lot of little things about our neighbors. Things I bet they will not tell and probably do not know I know. I keep my eyes open.

The census form was interesting. It was raining the weekend I filled it out—a nice quiet day to work on things like this.

I got in front of the fireplace. And everybody cried: "Move over. You're cutting off all the heat from the fire."

But I simply said: "Can't you see I am doing important work for the Government?"

It was very simple inside. Name. Male or female. Date of birth, etc. I liked the back better.

Do you have kitchen or cooking equipment? For use of people in your household only (those you listed in Section A).

That is a good one. I would like to explain that in person to the Department of Commerce.

We *do* have a kitchen. *And* cooking equipment for those listed in Section A.

Only we do not cook there—I suppose that is what they are getting at in this census.

We have a stove that cost $500. That was ten years ago

when the dollar was worth much more, and it took me ages to pay it off.

We have the stove. But we *cook* on a $9.95 barbecue.

We cook on the barbecue because it is more social in our set.

Is there a flush toilet in this house for use of this household only?

I would like to explain my answer to that one too.

The one in the bathroom upstairs has a bent wire or something. So you have to take the marble top off the tank and jiggle it a little. Then the rubber ball drops down and the tank fills. We keep intending to get a plumber over. But we get busy and forget. You know how it is.

Now, wait. *Downstairs.* That is important. Downstairs we have a flush toilet but it is *not* for those listed in Section A.

It is for guests. It is called "the downstairs powder room."

The downstairs powder room is *not* for those listed in Section A, because it is equipped with our best towels—the kind that are so thin you can see through them. And they get soaking wet if you touch them.

So nobody listed in Section A is allowed to go near the downstairs powder room. Especially just before a party. So I do not know if you can count this or not. I think our guests should list it in their Section A.

Now on this question, "Is there a bathtub or shower for the use of this household only?" There I would need to explain again.

There are both: But the bathtub is not for those listed in Section A. It is where the children exercise the guppies. Guppies are pet fish. They are supposed to be kept in a fishbowl. But the kids like to put them in the bathtub. Then they forget them and we have to net them out.

Except once in a while they put them in the flush toilet. So you can see, Mr. Census Taker, it is very complicated. And please drop around so I can explain exactly and keep my Government fully informed.

He staggered onto the morning commute bus and dropped his clanking fare in the box.

"Good morning, George," we said.

He raised his tear-stained eyes to us and gave a little choked sob.

"Her last words to me," he said, "(Boys, I'll cut my heart out if this isn't true!), her last words to me were: 'Just a slice of dry toast, Daddy. I'm on my diet.' "

"No need for alarm," we cried. "Dieting is normal in teen-agers."

"Not the diet," he said. "It was the way she said it. The syrupy, angelic, saintly little phony! I had to restrain myself from shying a saucepan at her head."

The morning commute bus is full of fathers. And fathers are full of woe. We are all in the midst of the diet craze these caloric days.

"She sits at the table," said George, "with a dial in her hand. She dials her dinner. One spoonful of carrots—75 calories. One bit of salad—25 calories."

"But," said George, "we do not dial or count the butter-scotch sundae after school—"

"Or," I said, "the bread-and-butter snack while doing the homework—"

"Does yours dip into each dish while she is setting the table? Like a chicken pecking corn?"

"Naturally. Also she seldom passes the icebox without scooping up a handful of anything loose."

I think we have been in the dieting stage for a year or a year and a half now. It seems longer. But it is the relativity principle—it seems longer when you are sitting on a red-hot stove.

It is not the dieting so much. It is the monotonous conversation.

Our daughters cannot add two and two for a score on the old report card. But they can dial calories into fractions and come up with immediate totals. Like a stage mathematician.

For a time we took all this quite seriously. Although our child looked like she was filling out in a normal way, she assured us she was disgustingly overweight.

(Curious thing is *all* these girls tell you the same thing. No matter what their various weights.)

We suggested a rugged course with Vic Tanny—Vic Tanny is a sort of chain-store gymnasium and reducing program that is spreading all over the world.

"Go to the Vic Tanny gymnasium and let them beat the lard off you."

Well, we *did* get a few of these young creatures into Vic Tanny's. And I guess the Vic Tanny people really whipped some fat off. Because they came out rather horrified.

"It's just like gym at school," they cried. "Only *more!*"

If there is anything we hate at school—anything we try to get out of with a passion—it is gym. Ugh!

The older ladies in the community get their lumps at Tanny's and come out slim. But it is too rugged for the younger generation, apparently.

Instead, we clip ads and read them to our fathers.

"You take these little tablets, see? And it says here that Gilda McGilch, the movie star, lost 13 pounds!"

That is the way we want to reduce. Pleasantly. Taking little tablets that movie stars take.

And dialing our calories. And with all of that, somehow we keep getting fatter and fatter and it is frustrating. Guess who it frustrates most? Climb on the bus, Daddy-O.

Love rules the court, the camp, the grove,
And men below, and saints above.

It is the season of love. There was a great outcry up on the hillside this morning. Up where we have the cowboy-and-Indian tent.

When I went out to see what was up, I found our son had tied up the four-year-old neighbor girl. He had her tied to a tree—not expertly but firmly. With a kind of pigging string I left up there.

He had a good explanation:

"She wants to go home and I don't want her to."

He was happy as could be and was making it pleasant for her.

"You can be a bear," he said. "Or an Indian."

The girl child did not want to be an Indian or a bear. She wanted to go home and get some bread with jelly on it.

I am happy to report our son stood fast. He just went right on hammering at tent stakes and little tent chores and let her weep. Let them have bread-and-jelly every time they want it, next time it will be mink coats.

I suppose this is some indication of love. Nobody has really got the word on love. Though poets have strummed the strings until it takes up two full index pages in Bartlett's *Familiar Quotations.*

All we really know is that it seems epidemic in the spring.

It is all over the daily paper. You locate love in the society section because it is a very social thing. PLIGHTS TROTH. PASSES CANDY. SETS WEDDING DATE.

With a teen-age girl in the house, we also keep up with Who's Whose in Hollywood. (We subscribe to movie magazines. The ones we can't afford, we go down and read off the rack at the drugstore.)

Currently we are keeping book on Marlon Brando. But cannot figure him out. We think he has not yet met the Right Girl; that is what we have decided.

Denis de Rougemont's book on love is marked down. To $1.95, I think. I saw an ad for it last Sunday and am preparing to purchase it.

Denis was a Swiss gentleman. He was sitting around the Alps or a bierstube or something, when he decided to study love.

He found love was not invented until the year 1150.

True. Until 1150 A.D., love was a matter of family trading. Or Boy meets Girl so what? I mean people did not give it the social oil we do today.

Love was started in the age of chivalry.

It was started by a bunch of knights.

These knights went around rescuing fair damsels and warming themselves by standing in front of fire-breath dragons. (For central heating had not been invented either.)

The Good knights beat the Bad knights. And you could tell the Good knight because he wore a fair damsel's gage in his helmet. (I am not sure what a gage was, but I think it was a garter maybe. It could not have been a garter belt because it would have fallen down over his eyes.)

Anyway, the Good knight wore the fair damsel's gage. He gave the Bad knight his lumps.

The King then inquired: "Sir Knight, why are you wearing that gage?"

The Knight thought about this in a chivalrous way. He was wearing it because all the other Good knights were wearing gages that season. But he had to have a better answer. So he said:

"Because I am in love."

Well, the word got around. And soon everybody was excusing what he did by saying he was in love.

And pretty soon the whole thing got out of hand and got on the social pages and there isn't a thing you can do about it.

With a good deal of grace and *savoir-faire* (if I do say so myself), we held down a chaperon position for the Junior Prom the other evening.

It is a nerve-racking thing—unless you get used to it, as Galileo remarked after they racked him up for the third time. A sort of subdued hostility radiates between the Chaperon and the Promenader. It is the relationship between the Player and the Umpire.

Says the Chaperon: "Good evening, Paul—I mean, John. Oh, Harry? Of course, yes. Hard to see in this light. Well, well, enjoying yourself?"

They gaze on each other uncomfortably.

Thinks the Chaperon: Heavenly days, these kids are younger than when I was in high school.

Thinks the Promenader: Gee, Mr. Hardshell sure looks funny in that outfit. I'm glad Dad didn't make me wear *his* tux tonight.

The evening then proceeds to deteriorate.

In all other ways it was a most successful affair. We contributed a teen-age daughter. She looked remarkably fresh, considering that it took an Act of Congress to get her dressed.

Most of the day was spent in preparation. A Roman orgy couldn't have taken more careful planning.

The young gentlemen were advised *not* to forget the corsages.

And the young ladies were advised *not* to order off the expensive side of the menu. "Take the regular dinner, not the de luxe. And *don't* order steak!"

Having thus enjoined the young to be frugal, the chaperons went out to the most elegant place in the county and belted down a champagne supper.

The duties of a chaperon are hard to describe. A chaperon has no textbook. Also no experience. (Once is enough.)

You read about these teen-age dances. And you hardly know whether to wear a carnation in the buttonhole or carry a bicycle chain.

However, decorum prevailed. Nobody seemed bent on stealing hubcaps or preparing for the Mafia.

We spotted our daughter dancing by. "Hello," we said timidly.

"Straighten your tie!" she hissed.

We all went down and straightened our ties. The mirrors in these locker rooms seem to age you. Have you noticed that? They ought to soften the light. Or something.

Anyway, considering how nervous we all were—we had three hysterics and one tantrum before we even got our hair up. Considering all that, the Prom was most successful.

I attribute a major part of this to the chaperons.

This is confirmed by the following all-day post-mortem. It was held via telephone. But we were not expecting any calls anyway.

The conversation was vague: "He *did?* Not *really!*"

But the interpretation is that it was a success.

One thing I imagine is bugging the French restaurant where the Promenaders had their dinner: Why did they all leave the little French peas on their plates?

"We ordered the regular dinner like you said. Only we were all afraid to eat the peas. We were so nervous, we thought they might spill off the fork and we'd just *die!*"

The suburban housewife is deeper than you think. Ask me how I know. Thank you.

The way I know is because the depth research people have been chaffering with the housewife. Mainly about their car problems.

"Six housewives of ten thought today's cars were too big," reports Dr. Freiberg, a man from Deepsville if there ever was one.

Many deep thinkers would have been satisfied with this. But the Doctor is no wader. He went right out to his neck. What about the other four?

"A number of those questioned volunteered that the streets are too small!"

Man, that is *deep!*

Well, this is all very interesting to your suburban correspondent. A study of the suburban housewife is always worthy—though right in this community a lady caught her husband studying suburban housewives. She got him twice with the old .38 before he could holler "ven."

Anyway, the Doctor studied these suburban wrens. And he came to the conclusion they were driving themselves daffy.

"She is the most overworked, underpaid chauffeur in the world. Each day she faces driving problems far more onerous than those which confront the average male driver."

The Doctor went on to list the problems: the school car poll; taxi-servicing the children; shopping and grocery delivery service; Red Cross meetings; church activities; delivering husband to bus and picking up same.

This was so fascinating that we decided to do our own study. We did not inform the subject housewife and imagine she will be surprised when she reads this.

We opened the study while subject and husband were having breakfast.

She: "Where did you put the car keys?"

He: "What do you mean, where did I put them? You were driving last night."

She: "Well, if you hadn't insisted on that last martini, you could have driven."

He: "Good grief! Are you going to start that again?"

This gives you a pretty good idea of what ladies are up against. Problems with the car even *before* they get into the car.

Only recently I decided to help the suburban housewife's car problems.

It is pretty obvious that one problem is backing out of the driveway. The car goes out of our driveway with *everybody* helping and giving advice.

"Watch out for the tree! Watch out, don't run over the child!"

In the meantime, the driver is gritting her teeth and backing like a maniac.

"Don't shout! It makes me nervous. Am I going over the flowers?"

Crash! Well, there goes the mailbox again.

It seemed to me, Sam, they made the plants to long. But since we cannot dig up the garden and make it all driveway, I got a smaller car.

The smallest car you can get is a German-made Isetta. It is a fine little car, about the size of a file cabinet. You would have to try hard to hit a tree with that car. It only takes five gallons every week or so and is a great saving to a frugal man.

Would you believe it, no suburban housewife wants to drive this car?

It is too short. And it is too light. And it doesn't park right because you can *see* where you are parking and we are used to parking by feel!

In fact, the best thing I can see about getting a little car is this: It does not help the suburban housewife. But is is a great help to the suburban houseman.

When things get too rough in the big car, hop in the small car and take off. Right, Doctor? Right.

We are in the midst of a battle of Man vs. Machine. To be exact, I am fighting with an IBM machine. I have followed the motto THINK—but find I cannot outthink the machine. I can't even get it to listen to reason.

We are in hock at the moment for $4.45. This is the IBM machine's price for a record called "Heavenly."

The disc is made by Columbia Record Club. Terre Haute, Indiana.

Having made the record, the Club turned the whole thing over to the Machine. The Machine never sleeps.

"Gentlemen," I wrote, "do not send anything. Stop billing me. Cordially, etc."

The Machine gobbled this up. Recorded, registered, spit out another bill.

I wrote again:

DEAR SIR: How is everything in Terre Haute? How is everything along the Wabash? I bet this will interest you: Many years ago our great-grandfather started from Terre Haute to dig gold in California.

Now your excellent company is trying to dig gold *out* of me in California. I thought you'd like that.

Why don't I want the recording of "Heavenly" you are asking yourself.

I don't have anything against the recording, heaven knows. (By the way, did they get the statue repaired in front of the courthouse? They were working on it when I was there last.)

I am sure the recording is a dandy. It is just that I cannot get our teen-age daughter to pay her telephone bill. Or return $2 she borrowed for hair spray. And I cannot see taking on $4.45 for the record. Just because she forgot to return the slip saying she did not want this month's selection.

If you have teen-age children, I am sure you will understand. (How did the cleanup job along the river go? They were doing a good job on it when I was in Terre Haute. You have a lively town there.) With best regards, etc.

I wrote this on the back of the punctured IBM card. Apparently, it did not get to the President of the Club. Not even a Vice-President.

The return card showed the familiar teeth marks of the IBM machine.

"Your statement was prepared on the date shown below. Payments, etc. $4.45."

DEAR FRIEND [I wrote]: As one rational human being to another—Wait! Don't put it in the Machine yet! Read!

I appeal to you as one normal person to another—

Now, look, blast it! What I mean is I have a daffy teen-age daughter who joined your record club. I know it states clearly that she doesn't *have* to take *every* record. She just takes three over the year.

The ones she doesn't want, she just returns the card.

The disheartening thing about this is she loses the return card. You say how is this possible? I tell you this kid lost *thirteen* fountain pens over one school year.

Now I ask you to settle this between gentlemen. "Comfort the afflicted"—I am sure you are a churchgoing person. Look at the situation with charity. We cannot go on this way. Yours truly, etc. (Terre Haute certainly looked like a prosperous town when I was there. I imagine $4.45 doesn't really mean much to you, does it? If you are ever out this way, look me up. We'd like to have you and the wife over for dinner.)

The answer has come back on the familiar punched card. There is no sign that it has received any more attention than the cold memory of the Machine.

I doubt that any human organization could do this to me. Terre Haute papers, please investigate! The Machines are taking over in your city! The President of Columbia Records is probably captive—if not already sacrificed.

Investigate! Investigate! Even now it may be too late.

10.

WE have spent years second-guessing Dr. Spock and Gesell. Believe me, we have had some interesting results.

Anyway, school ended the other day. Hallelujah!

It is our custom on such days to saunter down by the school, mitt the teachers and generally congratulate each other. On what, I don't know. Maybe that we have both come through the year without taking an ax to the children.

"We don't seem to have found her motivation."

The teacher tells me this with a patient little smile.

"How about the grades?"

"The grades could be improved. However, we find some children simply are not the scholarly type."

Well, this is no news to your scholarly correspondent. We have been going through final examinations. And I can tell you, we both need a long rest.

"Use the word 'burthen' in a sentence," she said gritting her teeth. "That is the next question."

"Are you using a stage Irish accent? There is no such word as 'burthen.'"

"There is so. It is right here in the book."

"It is a typo. A misprint."

"It is not."

That is the way we do our homework. Preparing for the finals.

Do you know there is such a word as "burthen"? True.

I reached for the dictionary. Just to show them. "Burthen. See Burden."

Now there is a word for you. "Burthen. See Burden."

"Why don't we just say burden? Like, 'Many a poor father finds his child a burden at examination time.'"

"I didn't make up the questions," she said sullenly. "If you don't help me, I will get a D."

We settled for "That blessed mood, in which the burthen of the mystery, in which the heavy and weary weight of all this unintelligible world, is lightened."

I got it out of Bartlett's *Quotations*. There was some chatter about "We are supposed to *make up* a sentence." But I shut her up on that.

I should make up sentences when Wordsworth has already done it for me.

"What is the next word?"

"Perigee."

"What?"

"Perigee."

"I never heard of such a word."

"It is that point in the orbit of a heavenly body nearest the earth," she read from the dictionary.

"Heavenly days!"

"Use it in a sentence," she said. "Otherwise I will get a D."

"Well, let me see. 'I can hardly wait for the perigee.' How is that?"

"I don't think it means anything," she said.

"I don't either," I said. "But maybe it will get the teacher off balance figuring out what it *might* mean."

Anyway, school is out. And we did not get a D. We are all looking for a little motivation. But have decided to put it off until next year.

Having worked on this project for years, I am in no hurry. I am patient.

I do not think this heavenly child is orbiting anywhere near the earth.

I think she is "at that point in orbit of a heavenly body farthest from the earth."

The word for that is "apogee."

Just in case you want to use it in a sentence.

Here I sit, full of flu and scarcely able to climb over the discarded Kleenex. Punished for my sins, expecially for bragging.

It seems during a gayer moment, I chattered about what a pioneer I was.

"Now that school is out, we will all go camping," I said grandly, "and sleep on the ground."

What gets into me anyway? To talk like that.

The point now is how to avoid the Outdoor Life—I think a whiff of outdoor life would end what little indoor life is left to me, that is my belief.

"I did not mean this week!" I cried. "Heavens-to-Betsy, I am a mere shell what with the flu bugs reaming me out.

"Even when I recover, I shall have to treat myself carefully for weeks and weeks. Convalescing slowly and carefully with my children bringing me broth and those pickles I love so well and—"

Well, it seems I *promised*. The son and heir is already in his Indian suit. And the dog has been washed for the journey. The minute I am better, the minute I can lift the gruel to my lips, everybody is ready to go.

I did a spell of camping in youthful and more resilient days. In those days I could sleep on rocks and they did not leave a dent in me.

No longer. I like a bed. In a house. A house with a heat-regulating device on the wall. It was in a nice house like this the other night that I recalled those golden days and made the rash promises.

"We slept right on the ground," I said. "And in the morning, you know what we did? We made bacon sandwiches. We packed them in our bags. And we went way upstream and fished down until dark.

"Then we cooked the fish and ate them."

I had everybody's mouth watering as I described the taste of trout over mountain mahogany coals.

I also recall that the mornings were brisk. And the water we waded in was fed by snow and was colder than billy-o.

If I have to do that again, they can start cutting off my dog tags.

The only thing that gives me hope is the march of progress. There has been a great deal more comfort in our lives in recent years. The camping dodge has not been neglected.

You can buy a tent with a screened-in porch for a couple

of hundred. And Abercrombie and Fitch will tuck you into a sleeping bag, warm down to 20 degrees below, for another C-note.

We have electric heaters and electric anti-insect lights.

The smart camper this year will carry a portable icebox, an air mattress and foam-rubber pillows. He will pack a folding washstand with a removable plastic bowl.

All of this would have horrified me when I was doing my stint with Nature. But now these things seem kind of natural —natural and *nice.*

"And can we make fire without matches? Like you said?"

"Did I say that?" I asked nervously. "Of course we will have to find a certain kind of wood—just the right kind of wood. However," I said happily, "if we do *not* find that kind of wood, the camping stores also advise that you carry a patent fire starter."

We must also take with us an ax. Though I have been looking at the ads. And do you know you can buy a whole bag of charcoal for practically nothing? Take that with you, add some fire starter and you get away from an awful lot of chopping.

"But we will sleep on the ground!"

Yes, absolutely. We will sleep on the ground, on which we will place the air mattress, the foam-rubber pillows, the sleeping bag of down. And possibly a Beauty Rest cot.

I am all for roughing it. But I've been sick lately.

Nature comes in on an expensive wave length these days. I stopped at a sporting goods store.

"I am taking a couple of children camping. What do I need?"

The storekeeper looked pleased.

"What do you have?" he asked. "You have an ax? A shovel? Sleeping bags? Camp-Pak dehydrated food?"

"We have nothing but stout hearts, Storekeeper. Stout hearts and the spirit of pioneers."

"Excuse me a minute," said the storekeeper. He went in the back room and telephoned. I could hear him faintly through the door. "I think you can get that mink coat after all, Mother," he said.

"Now," said the storekeeper briskly. "You must have this dehydrated food. Stews so delicious they melt in your mouth. Yet it weighs a pittance."

The stew came in a brown paper sack. It told you how you added water and all of a sudden, presto! You poured it out. *Coq au vin.*

"Couldn't I just buy food from the grocery store?"

"Why that would be cheating, wouldn't it?" said the storekeeper. "Now a nice sharp ax. Here is one imported from Italy."

"We just intended to pick up a few pieces of wood from the ground," I said timidly. "Or maybe rend a tree, limb from limb."

"Everybody has an ax," he replied sharply. "What are you going to wear on your belt?"

"My pants, Storekeeper."

"You should wear an ax, a compass and a whopping big hunting knife. Else," said the storekeeper, "how will people know you are a camper?"

I had never thought of it that way. I want people to think well of me. I bought it all.

"Now to the fishing," said the sporting goods man. "You must have rods and reels. Flies and fly-tying equipment.

And a handy little box to put them in. The box floats," he said, "in case you fall in the lake."

"I just thought I would cut a few poles. These children do not know the difference."

The storekeeper looked disappointed in me. But he was brave about it. He sold me a shovel. It was an excellent buy. (My boy dug a cunning hole that I fell into that night.)

The storekeeper sold me a compass. He sold me some hooks and some sinkers and a patent bobber that lands the fish for you.

"You wouldn't want an outboard motor, would you?"

"I have no boat, Storekeeper."

"I could order one from Los Angeles."

I said no thanks. He implored me to purchase a gun, a hacksaw, a folding tent and a packsaddle. But I was firm.

"Tot up the nudge, Storekeeper," I said. "For we are anxious to be out in the Great Outdoors. Sniffing the mountain breeze and the heady smell of wood smoke. And a trout frying in the pan."

"We have a nice pack of dehydrated trout with lemon dressing. Add a little water and—"

"I shall catch my own in my own wily way."

"Mosquito repellent?"

I bought some repellent. He urged a few lengths of rope on me. In case I wanted to hang clothing. Or myself. We bought a desert water bag.

It was expensive. But worth every dime of it. I went down the street, clanking with cups and knives and axes and compasses at my belt. People really stopped and stared.

"There goes a camper," I imagine they said. It costs money. But how else can they know what you really are?

✳ ✳ ✳

The witty trout have become gourmets. That is something I do not remember in my witty youth.

I cut three whippy aspens and tied line, leader and hooks on the end. I baited them with salmon eggs. The water was ice cold from the melting snow.

You could see a few trout in the quieter pools. But they only looked at the pink eggs. I don't know what they wanted —maybe for me to put it on toast with chopped egg and onion.

"The witty trout often do not feed until evening," I told the boy. "So you keep the line in the water. In case one of them wants a between-meals snack. And I will start a fire."

Do you know that places where people camp, there is hardly any wood? True.

Here we were in the very heart of a great national forest. Not a stick of wood.

"You should have bought the charcoal. Like the man told you," said my daughter. He *did* tell me to buy charcoal. I thought he was crazy.

"Never mind the criticism. Go get some wood."

That child is amazing. She came back with an armload. Cut to size.

"Where in the world did you get it?"

"Right over there."

There were some other people camped a few hundred yards downstream. They had a nice pile of wood beside their fire pit. Fortunately they were somewhere else. Fishing.

"Let us get the fire burning," I said hastily. "Before the people return."

Ordinarily I would not do this. But it may teach them a lesson not to hoard.

We dropped some new salmon eggs in the water. Yellow ones this time. You can get salmon eggs in all colors these days.

The witty trout just sat around laughing wittily at their own jokes.

They would not even eat salmon eggs when they fell off the hook.

The people who were fishing—the ones with the hoarded wood—came by. The man had a half dozen trout.

"They won't take salmon eggs," he said. "They only take worms."

"Where did you get the worms?"

"Down in town. They sell them in cans. Nice fire you got going there."

The fire with the borrowed wood blazed guiltily.

I put a pan on it and cooked some bacon. And we put in the trout that the nice storekeeper gave us.

And we all sat down and had dinner and agreed there was nothing like camping out. And living off the country.

"The Indians slept out on the ground all the time and were perfectly comfortable," I told my heir to our pioneer blood. "They didn't think it was cold."

"Co-o-o-o-l-l-l-d," he said, shivering.

"I'm freezing!" said my daughter.

Matter of fact, I was blooming near stiff myself. I don't see how the Indians did it. But I was giving a demonstration of camping out. Heavenly days, our pioneer blood is certainly getting thin.

All day we fished. (We did not catch any fish. But we gave them a good scare, I think.)

The sun warmed the pine needles and they gave off a fine

fragrance. The afternoon breeze rustled the aspens. There were a few snowbanks under the rock cliffs.

But when the sun dropped over the sawtooth range, the breeze came chilly off the mountain snow. The creek water was cold enough to make your teeth ache.

We slept in sleeping bags. I had forgotten how hard the ground is. There is always one buried rock that juts up and digs into you all night long.

Besides I had put the ax down in my bag—so the young woodsman would not arise early and chop off a leg. If I rolled off the rock, I rolled on the ax. And vice versa.

A cold full moon filtered down through the trees.

At 4 in the morning, the children were huddling for warmth. And I was thinking seriously of joining them.

"I'm dying," said my daughter. She had on all her sweaters and one of mine.

"Die quietly," I said, coldly. "Your own great-grandfather crossed these mountains. He never complained."

At least not that I can find out at this late date. "That night I slept a sweet sleep," he wrote in his diary in 1850. He was just a few miles south of here. Where the gold rush trail crosses Carson Pass at Tragedy Springs.

There is a monument up on the summit at 9,640 feet: "The highest point ever reached by the covered wagon. . . ."

I crawled out in the freezing dawn and threw a few sticks on the fire. I washed my face in the creek—it nearly killed me, but the moppets were watching. I considered shaving, but gave it up. I am not made of iron.

The children lay in the sack and watched me, moodily.

I cooked some bacon. I put the coffee on. It smelled wonderful.

The sun edged over Nevada and into California. The air began to warm and the breeze was softer. The offspring came out of their sleeping bag and stood around sniffing the breakfast. We tossed a fishline into the water. Just in case some trout felt lucky.

We then considered the whole situation—and I must say my children are considerate.

They *loved* camping, they said. They would *love* to stay more nights. On the hard ground. *But*— My daughter had just remembered she had a hair appointment. And the boy was worried about his toy fire engine. And—oh, a number of things.

"And if we drive down home today, Daddy, I'll cook dinner tonight."

So I let myself be persuaded. We drove over the Sonora Pass and down through the oak trees into the California valleys. I grumbled all the way about being dragged out of the rugged pioneer life. It was a pretty good act, if I do say so myself. O, pioneers!

The major problem with summer is that we must readust the allowance. I really don't know if I can face it again.

Fixing a budget for a teen-age girl is like fixing a leaky faucet. You know, you get one of these simple, guaranteed-to-work washers. You unscrew the faucet. You put in the washer, screw everything down again.

Whoosh! The water sprays out all around the edges. And the plumber makes all kinds of know-it-all remarks when you get him up.

Most of our allowance repairs are emergency.

"Can I borrow 50 cents? I'll pay it back out of next week's allowance."

Any father who would bring up the borrowed 50 cents again is considered a skinflint.

We went to work on the allowance about three months ago. The idea was that I was to clear all outstanding debts—like the books we forgot to take back to the library until there was a $3 fine on them.

I was to clear up all debts. We would start fresh.

We sharpened a lot of pencils. We told the small boy to go outside and shoot Indians with his cap pistol. I mean we approached the problem in executive fashion.

"Now we start with 25 cents for school lunch, right?"

"Yes, Daddy."

"Then we add 50 cents for entertainment."

"Yes, Father." (They are very polite when you are picking up their debts.)

"That includes shows."

"Shows? I *couldn't* do it for that. The show costs 65 cents."

"Okay," I said (The Last of The Big-time Spenders). "Make it 65."

I tell you, I worked up that budget in a way to make a CPA weep with envy.

I figured in tax rebates and fast write-offs. Petty cash and major disbursements and accounts receivable.

It came to $3.25 a week.

"And that is absolutely *all*. Okay?"

It was okay. She thanked me for my executive help. (She also borrowed 75 cents for wave lotion. But she explained it was an emergency.)

We all settled down, assured that the budget would run smoothly.

Naturally, I figured when school was over we should knock out a few budget items. Things like school supplies and lunches.

It seems it does not work like that at all!

"But you *promised* me $3.25 a week!"

There is absolutely no use arguing. I have pointed out the fallacy of such reasoning. How these items no longer exist. But no. The original amount is looked on as a legacy. Not only that, there are a lot of new things to be added.

You need *twice* as much wave lotion during summer on account of swimming. Did you know that? Well, you do.

The rare, warm days of June are upon us. The quail have nested on the hillside—at least I do not hear them calling these days.

A couple of weeks ago, they were noisy as could be. We could see pairs of them walking down the road. The male quail letting go with those three silver notes, promising a home in the suburbs and a new convertible. The female wearing that smug little look that females get when they have one man at the front door and another on the telephone.

It is a romantic season.

At this season of the year I get out the guitar. I sing. I sing melancholy, loving songs: "The Night the Firemen Came to Mother Kelly's."

When I sing and play on my guitar, a good many people around here get out of the house. They stand around looking irritable. Then they say:

"I think I have some shopping to do. Don't you have some writing to do today?"

That is an unkind thing to say. Of course I have writing to do. But I do not wish to be reminded of it.

I wish to sit in the sun and play single-string hot licks on my guitar. Tum-te-tum-tum-tum. That is a good one. I have been playing it over and over for an hour, I like it that well.

With a single-string hot-lick artist like me around, you would think people would listen. Not go upstairs and turn on the washing machine that drowns out all the hi-fi in my guitar.

The bluejays come down from the madrone trees. They sit in the sunlight and listen. A bird is musical and is impressed with a music man like me.

When we wind up the watch on the Rhine,
We will bind up two hearts that entwine.

That is a heart-buster. Get that "entwine." You drag it out—"en-twiiiiiiiinnnne." Wow!

"Yes, Sir, That's My Baby!" That is the first piece I learned on a guitar. I learned it on a ship running down the coast to Panama.

In the daytime I polished brass. Nighttime I practiced on the guitar and the Chinese deck crew held their hands over their ears. However, I became a virtuoso.

That is why I cannot understand why my daughter turns on the phonograph full-blast when I start to play the guitar.

She plays: "Tan Shoes—With Pink Shoelaces."

That is a crazy song.

I shut my ears to it. I will play my own music. The bluejay is quiet as a music major in the standing-room-only row at the Opera. A music lover.

I will play a few chords. A nice little progression of chords. Tum-te-dum-dum. Gets you right there, doesn't it?

He said to her right in the station,
I hope you reach your destination . . .

Here is a good piece: "There's a Dixie Girl Who's Longing for a Yankee Doodle Boy."

It seems to me songs were better in those days. I can hardly hear myself sing with that "Tan Shoes and Pink Shoelaces."

Tum-de-dum-dum-dum. *"Before she went away so far, he kissed her in the parlor car . . ."*

Well, everybody has gone shopping. Just me and the blue-jays. Music lovers. A day in June. And an eight-string Mexican guitar.

And a lot of talent. Do not forget that. What a day, what a peaceful day around the old family mansion. Too bad nobody hangs around to enjoy it. I simply don't understand that at all.